ADDITIONAL PR

ACTUALIZED TEAMWORK

In *Actualized Teamwork*, Will takes the many complex components of self-awareness and explains them in a way we can all understand. His approach and framework will provide you with the type of self-awareness necessary to become a more effective and resilient team leader who is comfortable and confident leading any group.

—**Steve Clifford**, *Charlotte Hornets*

Actualized Teamwork is the leadership book that needed to be written. With his insights into the interdependencies between leader style and team culture, Sparks provides a roadmap for how to build resilient teams that can consistently achieve ambitious goals. A must-read for anyone leading teams.

—**Jennifer LaClair**, *Head of Global Business Solutions, Fiserv, and Director, Whirlpool Corporation and the Federal Reserve Bank (Richmond)*

If you currently lead others or aspire to lead, you will benefit from Will's work. Perspective and self-awareness are difficult to ascertain and often hold many back from reaching their true potential. *Actualized Teamwork* is a must-read for anyone who wants to become the type of C-suite executive who can guide a best in class organization while also being an example for others to model.

—**Pete Guelli**, *Chief Operating Officer, Buffalo Bills and Sabres*

Dr. Sparks' decades-long research has explored two of the most critical components of organizational success—culture and teamwork. In *Actualizied Teamwork*, he translates his findings into insights for how leaders can optimize their team's performance and improve the long-term success of their organizations. I would strongly recommend this book to any leader who is committed to developing a high-performing team.

—**Dr. Pamela Davies**, *President Emerita and Professor of Strategy, Queens University of Charlotte, Director, Sonoco, and Board of Governors, Center for Creative Leadership*

Actualized Teamwork provides a powerful framework for understanding how leader styles and shadows create and reinforce team culture and performance. Anyone who is committed to becoming a better team leader should read this book.

—**Kim Henderson**, *Executive Vice President and Chief of Staff, Novant Health*

Building a world-class organization is done through building outstanding teamwork. The *Actualized Teamwork Framework* is the ideal tool for unlocking superior group effectiveness and ultimately, sustainable team and organizational performance.
—**Ken Walker**, *Partner, Falfurrias Capital Partners*

In *Actualized Teamwork*, Sparks provides critical insights on communication and trust—two elements that are often misunderstood or altogether missed by managers and leaders when establishing an identity and culture for their team. The real-world application makes this book a must-read for all leaders.
—**Daniel Eller**, *President, Ally Insurance*

Actualized Teamwork will take your self-awareness journey to the next level. Will provides the reader with a framework for creating the optimal balance between attending to both results and relationships. I recommend this book to any leader who wants to foster a dynamic culture and build high performing teams.
—**Michael Faulkner**, *President, Sealing Segment, Enpro Inc.*

Breaking new ground in organizational psychology, *Actualized Teamwork* introduces the transformative idea of team actualization and brilliantly operationalizes the concept of culture. If you are seeking to enhance the dynamics of your own team, or if you just want to understand the dynamics of groups and their broader impact, read this book!
—**Angela Yochem**, *Chief Information Officer, Krispy Kreme*

At Nucor, culture is our most important competitive advantage. In *Actualized Teamwork*, Sparks provides critical insights into how to measure and manage this foundational aspect of exceptional performance.
—**Donovan E. Marks**, *Vice President and General Manager, HR and Safety, Nucor*

Actualized Teamwork offers an integrated, research-driven approach for unlocking the process of exceptional team performance. Dr. Spark's framework reveals how to intentionally shape team culture, manage emotional dynamics, and achieve the synergy that comes from a sense of collective purpose and trust.
—**Dr. Shawn Bergman**, *Professor, Founder and Director of the HR Science Research Team, Appalachian State University*

In *Actualized Teamwork*, Dr. Sparks gives you unequivocal and highly pragmatic insights to foster the right team dynamics necessary to fully unleash the collective power and full innovative potential of any team.
—**Renato Derraik**, *Chief Information and Digital Officer, Live Oak Bank*

ACTUALIZED TEAMWORK

Unlocking the Culture Code for Optimal Performance

ACTUALIZED TEAMWORK

Unlocking the Culture Code
for Optimal Performance

William L. Sparks, Ph.D.

Society for Human Resource Management
Alexandria, Virginia
shrm.org
Strategic Human Resource Management India
Mumbai, India
shrm.org/in
Society for Human Resource Management
Middle East & North Africa Office
Dubai, UAE
shrm.org/mena

This publication is designed to provide accurate and authoritative information regarding the subject matter covered. It is sold with the understanding that neither the publisher nor the author is engaged in rendering legal or other professional service. If legal advice or other expert assistance is required, the services of a competent, licensed professional should be sought. The federal and state laws discussed in this book are subject to frequent revision and interpretation by amendments or judicial revisions that may significantly affect employer or employee rights and obligations. Readers are encouraged to seek legal counsel regarding specific policies and practices in their organizations.

This book is published by SHRM. The interpretations, conclusions, and recommendations in this book are those of the author and do not necessarily represent those of the publisher.

This publication may not be reproduced, stored in a retrieval system, or transmitted in whole or in part, in any form or by any means, electronic, mechanical, photocopying, recording, or otherwise, without the prior written permission of the publisher, or authorization through payment of the appropriate per-copy fee to the Copyright Clearance Center, Inc., +1-978-750-8600 or www.copyright.com. Requests to the publisher for permission should be addressed to SHRM Book Permissions, 1800 Duke Street, Alexandria, VA 22314 or online at https://www.shrm.org/about/copyright-permissions.

SHRM books and products are available on most online bookstores and through the SHRMStore at SHRMStore.org.

SHRM is a member-driven catalyst for creating better workplaces where people and businesses thrive together. As the trusted authority on all things work, SHRM is the foremost expert, researcher, advocate, and thought leader on issues and innovations impacting today's evolving workplaces. With nearly 340,000 members in 180 countries, SHRM touches the lives of more than 362 million workers and their families globally. Discover more at SHRM.org.

Library of Congress Cataloging-in-Publication Data

Names: Sparks, William L., author.
Title: Actualized teamwork : unlocking the culture code for optimal performance / William L. Sparks, Ph.D.
Description: Alexandria, Virginia : Society for Human Resource Management, [2024] | Includes bibliographical references and index. | Summary: "The first research-based book to introduce the term "team-actualization" and to operationalize the concept of culture, this book provides a straightforward assessment and methodology to measure and manage this often-elusive aspect of organizational life. The book identifies the 5 Dimensions of Teamwork and provides resources for teams to both assess and improve each key aspect of working in teams"—Provided by publisher.
Identifiers: LCCN 2024012396 (print) | LCCN 2024012397 (ebook) | ISBN 9781586446796 (trade paperback) | ISBN 9781586446840 (pdf) | ISBN 9781586446857 (epub) | ISBN 9781586446864 (kindle edition)
Subjects: LCSH: Teams in the workplace. | BISAC: BUSINESS & ECONOMICS / Leadership | BUSINESS & ECONOMICS / Human Resources & Personnel Management
Classification: LCC HD66 .S67828 2024 (print) | LCC HD66 (ebook) | DDC 658.4/022—dc23/eng/20240404

Printed in the United States of America

PB Printing 10 9 8 7 6 5 4 3 2 1

This book is dedicated to my mother, Linda Lee Sparks. Mom, thank you for being my lifelong role model for hard work, faith, and resiliency, and for never settling for less than my best.

In loving memory of my father, David Sparks.

Contents

Figures and Tables

Figures

Tables

Foreword

Ifirst met Will Sparks in the spring of 2014 when he was serving our organization as a leadership and group dynamics consultant. I spent time with Will as he led several sessions focused on organizational leadership and team culture. Later, over several ownership and management retreat meetings, Will led us in a number of exercises and discussions based on our assessment results that were designed to help us learn more about our individual and group leadership strengths and weaknesses. From my experiences with Will I knew that he could be a great asset for me and our coaching staff as we attempted to establish and sustain an effective and resilient culture for our basketball team. After that time, he worked with me as a trusted advisor.

Over the years the teams I have coached have always played above or below their collective skill and experience level, never at their actual aggregate level. While there are numerous factors that account for this observed outcome, what we often call chemistry—or what Will refers to as team culture—determines actual performance. My coaching staff and I are aways looking at ways to improve our general group culture and we decided that it could be worthwhile to bring Will in for a series of practices and get his thoughts on the dynamics of our team. He agreed, and after the practices we would sit down, and he would give me his impressions from what he had observed during our workout. He started with his thoughts on individual players and then gave me some ideas on everything from staff dynamics to practice structure. Will also had some recommendations on how we could improve individual and group work and culture. Some of his thoughts were structured in a way to help out in the short term while he also had ideas designed to improve our culture for the long term. I was amazed at how on target his general thoughts were regarding our players, and we immediately implemented some of his ideas.

I now speak with Will regularly to discuss leadership, group dynamics, and team culture. I utilize his background and depth of knowledge in each of these areas in attacking both individual and group challenges. Will has a terrific perspective on the type of culture we are trying to establish each season and constantly comes up with suggestions on how to improve our efforts. He has become an important asset for me, our staff, and our basketball team.

This book is a great read for anyone who is truly interested in learning more about themselves—which is where leadership starts. It is nearly impossible to set a definitive direction for a group and establish the type of connection necessary to have the buy-in from the players to follow you if you don't have a great understanding of who you are. In this book, Will Sparks will give you the opportunity to learn more about yourself, your leadership potential, and your impact on others as it relates to culture. As he always does, Will takes the many complex components of self-awareness and explains them in a way we can all understand. His approach and framework will provide you with the type of self-awareness necessary to become a more effective and resilient team leader who is comfortable and confident leading any group, whether a professional sports team, business unit, or entire organization.

—Steve Clifford, head coach,
Charlotte Hornets

Preface

I wrote *Actualized Teamwork* to help teams, groups, and organizations realize or actualize their highest collective potential. This process of a group of individuals reaching their highest collective potential, what I refer to as *team-actualization*, results in optimal performance and higher levels of personal satisfaction. This realization of collective potential comes from intentionally unlocking your team's culture code that underlies exceptional performance. To this end there are three major points I want to make from the outset that set this framework apart from other models of group behavior and team performance:

1. *Team-actualization*, much like self-actualization, is the process of reaching a group's highest collective potential by unlocking the team's culture code and managing the emotional dynamics of optimal performance. Sometimes referred to as *synergy* it is the result of a collective sense of purpose, trust, and engagement.

2. *Culture isn't just something that happens to you, you happen to it!* To some degree we all inherit the dominant culture, whether at the team or organizational level, of the enterprise for which we are working. However, we aren't just passive spectators in this dynamic. We contribute to the culture based on our Style and Leadership Shadow and, as such, we happen to it. The Actualization Team Profile (ATP) Framework identifies the emotional dynamics and resulting culture that your style and leadership shadow will likely help create and sustain.

3. *The ATP Framework has effectively operationalized culture.* The research underlying this effort has identified the benchmark scores (code) necessary for the optimal team performance.

Culture is often thought of as nebulous and difficult to define. The ATP Framework not only defines culture, it also provides the necessary roadmap to help you and your team achieve breakthrough performance by appreciating and managing the emotional dynamics and interplay of individual style and team culture.

Whether we realize it or not, we spend most of our lives in a group setting. Whether at work, our family unit at home, or our foursome on the golf course, we spend a significant amount of time in the company of others. If we adopt the British psychoanalyst Wilfred Bion's definition of a group as "three or more people who share a mental set," what we might refer to as a common goal, physical presence no longer becomes necessary to meet the definition of group or team. As my late mentor Dr. Jerry B. Harvey pointed out, even the hermit living alone is often doing so because of not wanting to be a part of a larger collective. And the more that person thinks about "them," even if it's in a "I'm-so-glad-I'm-not-a-part-of-that-community" sense, the more they are very much a part of their culture. In this sense, the definition of a group is greatly expanded to include all of us, from Zoom meetings to those living a life out of avoidance of others.

What's critically important for you, the reader, to realize is that even if you are not leading a work team, the concepts in this book will be relevant to you. The more time you spend in work team settings, whether in person or virtually, the more important the concepts, suggestions, and strategies outlined in this book will be to you. While some of the book does focus on the critical role that the leader plays in creating and sustaining culture, each individual contributes in some way and, as such, bears some responsibility for helping to improve the culture and performance of the group. This book will highlight specific strategies and techniques, what organizational psychologists often refer to as *interventions* to help facilitate positive change in Appendix E.

Moreover, this book is focused on helping you better understand that your style and your leadership shadow help create the culture you are currently experiencing in whatever group setting (e.g., work team, family unit, friendship group, etc.) you experience. While the culture of your group has an objective reality unique from the individual members, each member contributes to the culture. In other words, while we often want to lament and complain about our organization or team's culture as separate from us, we actually are deeply connected to creating and sustaining it. As the late Debbie Ford demonstrated, while we are pointing our index finger at "them" in order to assign blame, we must realize that our middle, ring, and pinky fingers are often pointing back at us.

Based on thirty years of research, including my dissertation at George Washington University, this book is my attempt to boil down everything I've learned and experienced in groups to practical, effective techniques and interventions to help you feel more engaged in your work group life and to help optimize your team's performance. Kurt Lewin famously said that "there's nothing more practical than a good theory." I can assure you that the concepts and team assessment, the *Actualized Team Profile*, presented in this book are based on years of research and the seminal theories of Carl Jung, Wilfred Bion, Jerry B. Harvey, Irving Janis, and many others. The reliability and validity statement may be found in Appendix H to establish the science behind this work. But perhaps more important than those statistics are the wry smiles, head-nodding, and gasps of "I've been on the road to Abilene!" that result from the face validity of concepts and frameworks that have immediate relevance and resonance to your own personal experience. Without that internal connection, this book will just represent another manual or approximate a textbook, only to be skimmed and quickly forgotten. I've tried my very best in the following pages to make sure your personal experience is the former, not the latter.

This book is organized into five parts or sections, which follow:

Part 1: Introduction and a detailed framework for team culture and group dynamics

Part 2: Overview of the three team shadow cultures: *Detached, dramatic* and *dependent*

Part 3: Review of the two classic pitfalls in group decision making: *Groupthink* and *the Abilene paradox*

Part 4: Exploration of team-actualization and the *5 dimensions of teamwork*

Part 5: Appendixes designed to help you optimize your team's performance and productivity, group decision making processes, and member engagement

Similar to my previous book, *Actualized Leadership: Meeting Your Shadow & Maximizing Your Potential*, I have interviewed organizational leaders from diverse settings such as financial services, energy, professional sports, and entertainment, to gain their expert perspective on building optimal team cultures, with specific focus on each of the five dimensions of team performance. These leaders who have graciously provided their expertise and insight into team performance are listed below in alphabetical order:

Jonathan Halkyard, chief financial officer, Metro-Goldwyn-Mayer (MGM) Resorts

Marlene Hendricks, chief customer experience officer, US Auto Trust

James Jordan, interim president and chief operating officer, the Charlotte Hornets

Kathie Patterson, chief human resource officer, Ally Financial

Brian Savoy, executive vice president and chief financial officer, Duke Energy

Also like my previous book *Actualized Leadership*, the primary psychological framework guiding this effort is a *psychodynamic* approach. This approach, which includes psychoanalytical (Freud) and analytical (Carl Jung) psychology, focuses on the importance of the unconscious or shadow in understanding and optimizing human behavior. The late British psychologist Wilfred Bion was the first to adopt this approach and apply it to group settings, exploring the impact that the collective shadow has on both group performance and individual engagement. The reason for using this psychodynamic approach, as opposed to others, is because in order for a team to realize its collective potential—*team-actualization*—its members must collectively confront and integrate their group shadow. Jung famously said that we can reach our highest potential and step into our brightest light only by "making our darkness conscious," not by "imagining figures of light." It's been my professional experience over the last thirty years that many team development efforts are grounded on "imagining figures of light," such as surface-level team-building and communication improvement efforts that not only fail to consider the team's culture and shadow, but actively prohibit it from being discussed. I've had more than one client tell me to "keep it positive" and to "focus only on the future" because addressing their culture would be uncomfortable for them. The result? Those sessions usually set the team backward—not forward—in their development. Thankfully I've reached a point in my career where I can politely decline those engagements. Refusing to acknowledge and accept our collective Sigmund shadow in a group setting has the same impact as for the individual who ignores, denies, represses, or projects their shadow. It keeps the person stuck, and further away from their ultimate potential. So, fair warning to the reader—if you open this process of team discovery and awareness there may very well be moments that are uncomfortable. Confronting the shadow, whether as an individual or a team, can be awkward and difficult. But I promise you this: it is worth every second of awkward silence or emotional outbursts. It is only through this process of recognizing and integrating our collective shadow that we can truly build trust, connect with others on a deep level, and experience peak performance and teamwork that is in the zone that comes from team-actualization.

So let's get started. If you haven't already done so, please complete my short, free assessment (free Actualized Team Profile [ATP], short form) which may be found at http://www.atpfree.com.

If you are interested in having your team complete the full ATP that includes your culture code, please contact us at www.actualizedperformancesolutions.com.

Your survey results will help you better connect to your primary leadership style, corresponding leadership shadow, and the resulting team culture (*detached, dramatic,* or *dependent*) that you are most likely to experience, either as the leader or a participant in a group setting.

We need to start with the practical foundation of a "good theory" that Kurt Lewin emphasized, and that table will be set in Part 1, Chapters 1 and 2. And just like in *Actualized Leadership*, my introduction to, and appreciation for, group dynamics starts with the late Dr. Jerry B. Harvey. Up until my first doctoral seminar taught by Dr. Harvey, I had only read about concepts related to small group behavior and organizational dynamics. But in Dr. Harvey's class we were going to have much more than an intellectual experience learning about group dynamics and culture. He was going to make sure we had an *emotional* experience in order to *feel* these concepts play out in a very real and meaningful way.

Acknowledgments

According to Wilfred Bion, all behavior is group behavior. His contention is certainly true with this book as it represents a real team effort. There are so many colleagues and friends that, for me, meet Wilfred Bion's definition of a team "sharing the same mental set" that I want to recognize and thank. First, I want to thank John Repede, my friend, business partner, and colleague of over twenty years for your technical savvy, creative insights and much needed sense of humor. Because of your rare blend of expertise and creativity, I often refer to you as a *mathamagician* who has made me a better researcher, teacher, and consultant. My business partners Jane Williams and Erika Weed continue to challenge me and my thinking, and our synergy as a firm is a testament to actualizing collective potential.

Linda Vespa is an editor-extraordinaire that I have had the good fortune of working with over the last twenty years, and here's to twenty more. Steve Codraro is a gifted graphic designer with an uncanny ability to graphically illustrate complex concepts with creative yet simple insight.

Joe Pieri's research establishing the statistically significant correlations between leader style and team culture is, in my humble opinion, one of the most important contributions to the fields of organizational behavior and psychology in the past decade. The continued research efforts of Kayshia Kruger and J.C. Fedorczyk on Actualized Performance, resiliency and team dynamics continue to help evolve and expand our model of human potential and team performance.

I am indebted to my mentors Peter C. Browning, Pamela Davies, and John Lobuts, as well as the late Jerry B. Harvey and Dominic J. Monetta, for taking an interest in me and, in doing so, changing my life. I also want to thank my colleagues and friends Ken Walker, Kim Henderson, and K.C. Woody who continue to inspire and challenge me.

I am grateful to my family for their ongoing love and support. Thank you to my wife, Erin, and our son, Bennett, who remind me daily of dynamic synergies that can, and often do, occur in our family unit. Thank you to my mom Linda Sparks, my brothers Wade and Bert, my sister-in-law Carolyn, my brother-in-law John, my in-laws Randy and Robyn Stump, and our Cavapoo Shelby "Scooter" Sparks, for helping me remember what matters most.

I especially want to thank Matt Davis, Montrese Hamilton, and Ashley Miller at SHRM for their ongoing support, feedback, and encouragement.

Finally, I am grateful for the good music over the years that includes Fleetwood Mac, U2, Steely Dan and Rush, as well as my new indie favorites Daughter, the Paper Kites and Bon Iver, that keep me company during the early morning and late evening hours of writing (and re-writing).

Now that's a team effort!

Introduction

Since the beginning of time, human beings have needed each other in community to survive and thrive. We each bring our own unique, lived experiences and perspectives, both good and bad, to this world. Respecting and managing this diversity of thought in context of teams creates the opportunity for collective creativity, innovation, and action to reach a common goal. If done right, it contributes to the intrinsic satisfaction of group members while also driving effective performance for the team. If done wrong, it derails alignment and productivity of the group working as a team to reach short and long-term goals. That is why it is so important for leaders to create a group culture that cultivates safety and trust, promotes self-awareness, and provides effective ways to communicate.

Over my twenty-five years working in Corporate America, I have led an array of teams. Earlier in my career I was exposed to Will's framework for understanding how both individual and group shadows adversely impact performance and satisfaction. I learned that while maximizing my strengths is important, understanding my deepest fear or leadership shadow and how it shows up in different situations is critical. There is a well-known adage that "we are wounded in community, and we are healed in community." Our experiences in group settings and teams often create the space to share, learn, grow, and heal. Immediately, with this new knowledge, I noticed that my approach to leading teams had changed. I still made it a priority to understand the strengths of the team, but I was also intentional about creating a safe environment for the team to be vulnerable and open up about things they were managing through. This type of group culture fostered trust, built confidence, embraced transparency, and encouraged effective collaboration and teamwork. For more than a decade I have led teams with this awareness and approach, and as a result I have increased employee engagement, optimized teamwork, surpassed performance goals, and been promoted as an executive to solve global problems. None of this would have been possible without me understanding how to manage my leadership shadow while using my platform to be transparent, authentic, and courageous enough to encourage others to do the same.

I have personally known Will for over a decade and his passion, dedication, and commitment to providing resources that help leaders strive to reach their highest potential has been the gift that keeps on giving. In fact, we coauthored and published "Toward a Comprehensive Theory of Personal Transformation" in a peer-reviewed journal as an outgrowth of our mutual interests and work together.

In his newest contribution, *Actualized Teamwork: Unlocking the Culture Code for Optimal Performance*, Will has masterfully created a framework that connects and informs leaders across all generations and levels of management on how to better understand the impact that their leadership style and shadow has on team culture and performance, along with ways to drive the best results through optimal teamwork. If you are looking for a book to empower and provide a mechanism to help teams collaborate and work in a unified way, look no further!

—CaSondra Devine, head of supplier diversity
for Worldwide Amazon Stores, Global Procurement

PART I

THE WISDOM OF
TEAMS?

Chapter 1

Group Dynamics 101

What's in this chapter?

- » The Wisdom of Teams?
- » The Curse of the Crowd?
- » Group Dynamics 101
- » Practical Takeaways from a Theoretical Course
- » What's Next

The mentality of groups is not that of individuals.

—Emile Durkheim

THE BIG IDEA

Experiences in teams range from synergistic performance to frustrated detachment, and everything in between. The culture of the team, which is often an extension of the leader's style and shadow, determines both the short-term intrinsic experiences of team members as well as the long-term performance. Culture is difficult to spot, and even more challenging to manage and improve.

Our experiences in groups are so varied and vastly different that it's hard to quantify exactly how it feels to engage in group dynamics. As a sort of take on the traditional definition of pornography, when it comes to peak performance and synergy, *you know it when you see it*. But what about *groupthink* or the feeling of frustration or even exasperation that so many of us experience in group settings, whether at work or at home?

In the classic *The Wisdom of Teams*, authors Jon Katzenbach and Douglas K. Smith extol the virtues of working in groups and the synergistic decision-making and problem-solving processes in groups that consistently outperform those processes in individuals. But is there really *wisdom* to be found in teams? In *The Delusions of Crowds: Why People Go Mad in Groups*, author William J. Bernstein explores group behavior and reaches very different conclusions about the quality of output and performance of groups. So, which one is it? Is there "wisdom" to be found, or are we cursed to "go mad"?

I think those are profoundly important questions to ask ourselves. In a world where we have recently witnessed incredible social upheaval and rioting from Seattle, Washington, to Washington, DC, and many, many towns and cities in between, coming to grips with the forces that underlie group dynamics and behavior is crucial. But here's the thing: you don't have to participate in a riot on the one hand, or a championship team on the other, to have some sense of group culture and the resulting behavioral dynamics that occur. Whether in our family unit, workplace team, or foursome on the golf course, we can all relate to group experiences that have both been positive and energizing, and negative and frustrating.

The Wisdom of Teams?

In the early 1990s, authors Katzenbach and Smith published one of the best-selling business books of the decade, *The Wisdom of Teams*. In this book the authors extol the virtues, optimal decision making, and performance that occur in groups. In fact, the authors state that the reason groups are preferable to individual contributors is their evolution into high functioning teams, claiming "groups become teams through disciplined action. They share a common purpose, agree on performance goals, define a common working approach, develop high levels of complementary skills, and hold themselves mutually accountable for results. They never stop doing any of these things." Other likeminded books such as *The Diversity Bonus* (Page 2017) and *Smart Leaders, Smarter Teams* (Schwarz 2013) promote the findings that working in groups, as opposed to individual efforts, is more creative and ultimately more productive, and that we should both seek out and relish the opportunity to work in groups.

What's your reaction to their perspective? Having taught Master of Business Administration (MBA) classes for almost thirty years, I can tell you that the most consistent complaint I get from my students is the portion of the class dedicated to group projects. Students feel like they are often putting their "A" at risk with having to partner up with other students to complete an assignment that, truth be told, many students would rather work on alone. I think that feeling carries over into many arenas in our lives, from work settings where we have a fast-approaching deadline, to family outings where the desire for consensus and compromise outweighs optimization, meaning that we end up with a decision that we all live with, but no one is willing to die for. This dynamic often occurs when a couple or family is sitting in a restaurant on a Saturday night that no one really wants to be at.

The Curse of the Crowd?

In 2021, author Bernstein published *The Delusion of Crowds: Why People Go Mad in Groups* as a critical and cautionary tale of the dynamics that occur in groups. Using historical examples to illustrate his point, he reminds us of Sigmund Freud's important insight when it comes to group behavior: group feelings are always simple and exaggerated and can contain only the extremes of either love or hate. Building on the seminal works of Gustav Le Bon, Bernstein reaches a similarly negative conclusion about group behavior. Namely, he summarizes the biological and psychological reasons that groups maintain beliefs and convictions despite objective facts and evidence to the contrary and, in doing so, illustrates their inability to effectively manage nuance, ambiguity, and subtlety.

Whether you subscribe to the notion that group work more often produces wisdom, or that group life usually feels more like a curse, it does appear that the French sociologist Emile Durkheim was indeed correct when he pointed out that whether your experiences are extremely positive or extremely negative, the mentality of groups is different than the mentality of individuals.

So, we are back to asking our original question: Which one is it? Some experiences are so uplifting and produce a sum greater than the individual parts (i.e., synergy), while other experiences in groups lead to frustration and poor (even catastrophic) decision making (e.g., the National Aeronautics and Space Administration [NASA] decision to launch Challenger in 1986). I think the question we need to ask is why? Why are some experiences so uplifting and others so frustrating?

The answer to which one is it is both, and the reason to why is culture. Experiences in groups are both positive and synergistic, and negative and exhausting. And culture—the underlying atmosphere of the group—determines the experience. Much like individuals have unique personalities, groups, teams, and organizations have cultures—the unique style of a group. Culture manages the *how* or process for the *what* or task. We spend so much time focusing on the *what* and *when* instead of investigating the *how* and *why*. For example, individuals who successfully lose weight and commit to a healthier lifestyle don't just ask what they want (to lose weight) and when (before my next vacation). They also focus on the how and why: why do I overeat (triggers) and how can I create new, healthier habits? Likewise, teams that experience synergy, wisdom, or diversity bonuses attend to both: what and by when they need to accomplish, why they are focused on this task (e.g., their mutual purpose, etc.), and how they will work together (e.g., ground rules, team commitments, etc.).

Group Dynamics 101

In my last book, *Actualized Leadership: Meeting Your Shadow & Maximizing Your Potential*, I referenced the late Dr. Jerry B. Harvey and the "F in Life" he gave me in my first semester with him. What I failed to mention was that the reason I took his feedback to heart, and in fact one of the reasons he was so respected and revered, was his approach to not-teaching. Now, you may be wondering why a renowned professor and author, a retired Professor Emeritus at George Washington University, would be applauded for not doing what he was paid for: teaching. That's a fair question, and frankly one that his first-year students pondered quite often.

Well, the reason was because Dr. Harvey didn't want simply to cite authors, as well as his own work, and then have students regurgitate the right answer back on a quiz. He figured you can get that in any graduate program. His goal was to create the conditions, which often included more than a little anxiety, so that you could actually feel the subject matter. Giving a lecture would, in his view, actually inhibit learning.

Dr. Harvey had famously described *the Abilene paradox*—a common experience where groups and teams are unable to manage their agreement and, as such, make decisions that no one really supports—and agreed with the small group behaviorist Wilfred Bion (discussed in the next chapter) that the most common emotion experienced in group settings was frustration.

But it wasn't enough to just tell us that. No, he wanted us to experience it.

So, in our very first group dynamics course, "Human Factors in the Process of Change," he came into the classroom at exactly 4:30 p.m. when the class was scheduled to start. The chairs had already been arranged in a circle and he took the last remaining chair. After settling into his seat, he slowly looked around the room, sighing somewhat dramatically after making (or attempting to make) eye contact with each of us. After what seemed like a very long pause,

Dr. Harvey said, "Well, welcome to 'Human Factors in the Process of Change.' My name is Jerry Harvey and I'm your professor. So, what are we here to do?"

Silence. Total, awkward silence.

Ruth, a student in this class, cleared her throat and said we were here to learn from one of the most esteemed professors about experiences in groups. Dr. Harvey replied, "I've got nothing to teach you." Continuing on, he said, "So, let me ask this again, what are we here to accomplish?" Silence. No one dared follow Ruth in her well-intentioned but failed attempt to break the ice. "God almighty," exclaimed Dr. Harvey. "What was the Admissions Office thinking when they admitted this cohort?" With that, Dr. Harvey picked up his briefcase and walked out of the class.

Silence ensued, followed with comments in the general vein of "what the hell was that?" Amy, another student in the class, quickly assessed that one of our textbooks was Dr. Harvey's own *The Abilene Paradox: And Other Meditations on Management* and that we should have been prepared to discuss his work. We all agreed, and we spent the next week reading and re-reading his book, ready for the next class.

Second class, 4:30 on the dot, same circle of chairs, and an exasperated Dr. Harvey sat down and said, "Okay, let's try this again. What are here to do?"

Amy, brimming with confidence, exclaimed, "Dr. Harvey, I am here to ask you about your 'meditation' in Chapter 4 regarding Abraham and Issac, and why ..." but Dr. Harvey interrupted her. "Brown-nosing your professor won't work, at least not with me."

Silence.

Long, awkward, silence.

Dr. Harvey got up, walked out, and this time slammed the door a little louder.

After this experience, the entire class as a whole got up, walked over to the TGI Fridays in Foggy Bottom, and over several rounds discussed what the hell was going on in this class. A couple of classmates had calculated their tuition by number of class sessions and by their estimate they were not receiving a very good return on a quite expensive investment. But Gene, an insightful, creative, and courageous student, surmised that perhaps this experience— this frustration and debate over beers—was the class. Perhaps, he mused, that we weren't going to be graded on content. Rather, we would be evaluated on our ability to learn and grow in this class that was more of an experimental lab than a traditional class. Perhaps we would be graded on our ability to collectively manage our anxiety and frustration as a class. I think I quipped something sarcastic about failing to secure my white lab coat for this "lab," but deep down, I had a feeling Gene was on to something. And I assured Gene that I would be right behind him the following week when he served as our spokesperson.

The third class meeting. Dr. Harvey again came in at 4:30 p.m. on the dot but this time he didn't sit down, claiming he was getting too old to get up and down, and, given his very low confidence in this class's ability to adapt to his not-teaching approach, said, "I'm going to ask you one last time, 'Why are we here?'"

Gene, mildly irritated and also a little nervous, said, "Why are you doing this to us?" Dr. Harvey, in his first real moment of engagement with the class, said, "Doing what? What am I doing to you?" Gene continued, "You are making me and all of us feel very uncomfortable and frustrated. Why are you creating so much anxiety?" Dr. Harvey retorted, "I'm not creating anything! Your frustration with me is because your unrealistic expectations and need for a co-dependent professor are not being met and you're taking out your irrational psychopathology on me!" He then walked over to the whiteboard and asked, "How does everyone feel right now? Just shout it out."

With that invitation, and an almost unanimous agreement around frustration, anxiety, irritation, fear and the like, our class started. As Dr. Harvey captured our output on the whiteboard, it became more obvious with each emotion written down what immature and unrealistic expectations we had. Moreover, we realized that, as a class, we were colluding in a negative fantasy of needing an all-knowing leader to teach, which as Dr. Harvey later pointed out, is a pretty lousy model for how mature humans actually work, learn, and live.

And in that moment of our third class, our eyes (and hearts) were open to what Dr. Harvey was trying so desperately to not-teach us: when we project our own unconscious needs for protection, direction, and support onto most group settings, and they are not met (i.e., Dr. Harvey refusing to teach), we feel frustrated and exasperated. But here's the thing: it's our own individual psychopathology and unconscious needs, what Wilfred Bion refers to as our *basic assumption mental states*, that create this experience. I've spent the better part of the last twenty-five years researching team development and group work in both corporate and academic settings, and this pattern repeats itself over and over again. Whether groups of individuals gather in a classroom, meeting room, or dining room, the same unconscious forces appear and attempt to take over the group.

And that's when the light came on for me and most of the class, and the cost of tuition was worth it one hundred times over, the first two missed classes notwithstanding. In a group setting, it's the combination of all of members' unconscious needs in the aggregate—what I call the shadow—that causes so many problems. Only when a group or team manages this aspect of group life, the *how* and the *why*, can they then effectively optimize the *what* and the *when*.

Practical Takeaways from a Theoretical Course

Although this course in group dynamics focused on theory, a lot of theory, there were many practical takeaways and useful insights that I still employ today in my classrooms and consulting practice. Although different situations and different team dynamics call for different interventions and approaches, the following practical takeaways inform my approach in working with teams and organizations:

» A psychodynamic theory of group behavior works. First and foremost, psychodynamic theories and the resulting acknowledgment and appreciation for the power of the collective shadow has great utility. Recognizing this aspect of group life is a critical first step toward true and sustainable team development and growth. At the end of the day, it works; this approach produces positive and lasting change and results.

» You do not have to be a psychoanalyst or a psychologist to use this framework. While the name psychodynamic may create visions of a patient on a couch discussing their childhood experiences to a distant and clinical analyst, you do not need extensive training in order to identify and integrate the collective shadow components of group life. Bion identified the reoccurring and universal patterns of group behavior, and the Actualized Teamwork Profile (and the free assessment, http://www.atpfree.com) is designed to provide you with the framework you'll need to help your team shine some light on your collective shadow.

» Experiences in groups, while they feel unique and sometimes even personal, are universal and, as such, predictable. For many of us, past negative experiences in groups feel specific to an issue or another personality, and the resulting exchanges (e.g., conflict, mismanaged agreement, etc.) feel very personal. I can assure you they are not. The *Actualized Teamwork Framework* is designed to help you identify your culture, and the specific underlying shadow beneath it, as well as likely decision-making dysfunctions that may be impacting your specific culture. With this new insight, you are much better able to predict and manage these potential negative outcomes. In short, the framework allows you to take something that is murky and unseen (and by definition, unconscious), and better manage team dynamics.

» Teams can develop, grow, and improve their culture with focused efforts. Allowing team members to acknowledge fear, frustration, and the like is a powerful first step in acknowledging their collective shadow. We all have an inherent need to confront reality without fear of reprisal. At that moment, the team begins to create a more dynamic culture because the group shadow retreats. Failing to confront reality and have candid, honest communication with the team (e.g., just wanting to stay positive or focus only on the future, etc.) feeds the group shadow, giving it even more power and influence over the team.

»   Teams that spend time on the process are more effective at their task. That seems counterintuitive when a team is running up against a deadline or under enormous pressure for a deliverable, but savvy leaders and insightful members understand the tremendous power that comes from spending some time on process—the *why* and *how* of the given task. I know it can be challenging to schedule an offsite retreat or even to take twenty minutes at the beginning of each meeting to center and allow members to check-in, but that allows the team to collectively exhale and come together in an authentic way, while also allowing members to be mindful and present for the meeting. For leaders and teams who tell me that they are too busy to adopt this practice, I remind them about the wise adage of the Buddha who recommended that his pupil meditate for thirty minutes every morning. When the pupil exclaimed that he knew that was important but was just too busy to commit to that amount of time, the Buddha is reputed to have said he completely understood. And in that case, he recommended that he meditate for an hour instead.

What's Next

Chapter 2 presents the *Actualized Teamwork Framework* and provides an overview of the theoretical foundations for the model. Specifically, the *Actualized Teamwork Framework* employs a psychodynamic model for understanding group dynamics and is focused on both diagnosis (description) and treatment (prescription) by combining both the psychoanalytical and humanistic perspectives in this model. Based primarily on the work of Wilfred Bion, the framework describes the three shadow team cultures and their corresponding leadership styles: *detached* (*achiever*), *dramatic* (*affirmer*), and *dependent* (*asserter*).

Chapter 2

Actualized Teamwork: A Framework

What's in this chapter?

» Team Culture versus Organizational Culture
» The Psychodynamic Perspective of Team Culture
» The *Detached* Culture and the *Achiever* Style
» The *Dramatic* Culture and the *Affirmer* Style
» The *Dependent* Culture and the *Asserter* Style
» What's Next

The taboo against believing in the existence of a social entity is probably most effectively broken by handling the entity experimentally.

—Kurt Lewin

THE BIG IDEA

Teams often regress to primitive states based on the collective instinctual impulses of the members. Under stress, they often allow the unconscious, shadow side of group life to dominate the team's dynamics. When this occurs, rational and objective decision making, open communication, and mutual accountability yield to irrational and subjective decision making, self-censorship, and overreliance on one individual for direction.

Actualized teamwork refers to realizing or *actualizing* the inherent, synergistic potential of a group. Synergy is often defined as the sum being greater than the individual parts. In other words, when a team of three members actualizes their collective potential and achieves synergy, 1+1+1=4 (or 5 or 6 or some number greater than 3). For example, when a sports team with less talent on paper manages to pull an upset and defeat the team with superior talent, we often invoke the term *chemistry* to describe the underdog's performance in achieving victory. That dynamic—the team achieving more than what would have reasonably been expected based on the individual parts—is the synergistic effect at the heart of team-actualization.

In my book *Actualized Leadership*, the central aim that I was trying to convey was that for individuals to maximize their potential, they had to have the courage to face their own individual darkness. In fact, that book's subtitle is "Meeting Your Shadow & Maximizing Your Potential." Likewise, the same notion holds true for teams and groups. In order for a team to achieve its collective potential—*team-actualization*—the team members must have the courage to face the collective shadow that resides in their unique culture. In an oversimplified sense, consideration for the hidden or unconscious element of human behavior is the essence of a psychodynamic approach. In order to understand observable behavior at the individual or group level, we must appreciate the hidden aspects of the unconscious forces driving behavior. Freud referred to these unconscious forces as the id, and Jung called it the shadow. For our purposes, we will refer to this component of team performance and group dynamics as *culture*. And in the same way that an individual's personality contains an unconscious (the id or shadow) component, the culture of a team or group contains their collective shadow component as well.

Social scientists have long recognized the existence of the concept of culture as it relates to group dynamics, decision making, and performance. Research from such diverse fields as psychology, sociology, anthropology, education, public administration, management science, and my field, organizational psychology, provide ample evidence of the existence of something different and more than the collection of individual personalities. This something which I refer to as team culture has also been referred to as group atmosphere, syntality, the collective mind, and stage of development, just to name a few. For our purposes going forward, I will use the term *team culture* to describe this quality of being. Team culture is defined as follows: *The perceived attitude and group dynamic that results from the dynamic interplay between the overt task and the collective group shadow.*

Figure 2.1 illustrates the concept of culture using the common iceberg metaphor. In this conceptualization, there are three unique aspects to culture: (1) observable behaviors and artifacts above the surface of the water; (2) dimensional norms and values that guide behavior exist both above and below the surface of the water; and (3) collective shadow of the group that is unconscious and operates on a tacit (as-if) level.

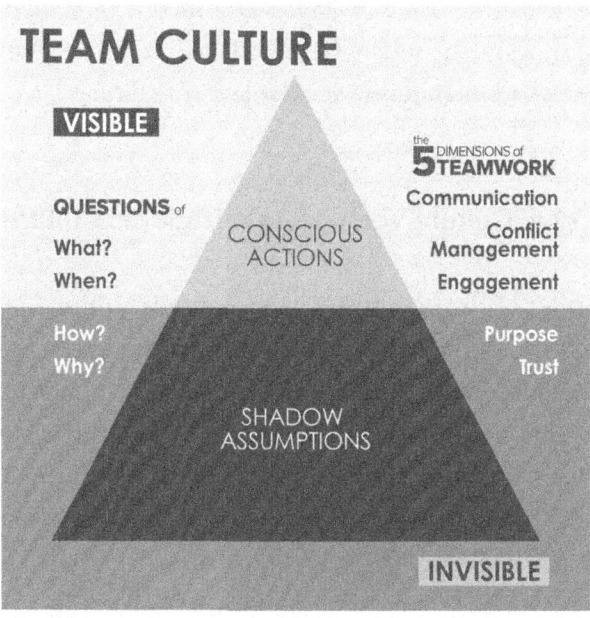

Figure 2.1. Team culture illustrated

» **Observable behaviors and artifacts:** The patterns of communication, decision-making, and conflict management processes that are unique to a team, as well as what behaviors are rewarded or reinforced, and what behaviors are punished or ignored. Artifacts include the team's logo, mission statement, dress code, and formal hierarchy that resides within the team.

» **Dimensional norms and values:** The unwritten rules of engagement that reinforce expectations, including the more deeply held convictions about what is good, bad, desirable, undesirable, and the like. *The 5 dimensions of teamwork* exist both above (*communication, conflict management,* and *engagement*) and below (*purpose* and *trust*) the surface. Essentially, these elements of culture are made explicit when rationales and justifications for certain acts are used and decisions are made.

» **Collective shadow:** The deepest level of culture that is unconscious and can be surfaced only through deep discovery, vulnerability, and awareness. The tacit or as-if assumptions about the team and its larger environment reside here, and lead to group behavior that is often in reaction to someone or something. Primal issues such as scarcity, abundance, fear, safety, and survival are grounded in this deepest level of culture.

Team Culture versus Organizational Culture

It is important to distinguish between the team culture and organizational culture. While the two are related and may even be very similar, they are different, separate, and unique. A metaphor that I often use to describe the differences between the two is the comparison between the national weather map (organizational culture) and your local weather forecast (team culture). The term *culture* was first used by the late Elliott Jaques (who also coined the term *midlife crisis*) in 1951 to describe the shared assumptions and observable patterns of behavior in a manufacturing environment. Perhaps the name most associated with organizational culture is Edgar Schein, whose seminal work in this area led to an appreciation for culture existing at multiple levels. Schein also explicitly noted the unconscious element of culture, which he referred to as *underlying assumptions* and *basic assumptions* as the most difficult yet most important element of culture to manage. Influenced by Schein, numerous other organizational researchers, including Manfred Kets de Vries, Robert Quinn, and Daniel Denison, highlighted the importance of identifying the unconscious or shadow elements of an organization if you are going to successfully transform the corporate culture.

But back to our metaphor explaining the differences between the two: organizational culture exists as the national weather system for an entire organization and may be best thought of as the season of the company: spring, summer, fall, or winter. Team culture, on the other hand, emerges as both a part of the larger organizational culture and as a unique dynamic for a specific group (e.g., department, division, board of directors, etc.) of individuals, and exists as your local weather. It often complements the national weather map, but at times it can be very different at the local level. I cannot count the number of business leaders I have coached and consulted with over the years who were very skilled at creating pockets of desirable weather—often against a very challenging national weather season—which greatly helped propel them on to greater levels of success and satisfaction.

We've already defined team culture as *the perceived attitude and group dynamic that results from the dynamic interplay between the overt task and the collective group shadow,* and I would like to expand on that notion briefly to encompass some critical artifacts of group behavior, such as

» Patterns of communication,
» How information is shared,
» How problems are solved,
» How decisions are made,

» How opportunities are captured, and

» Level of engagement and satisfaction of group members.

So far, we have defined team culture and compared it to organizational culture. Before we review some of the most important psychodynamic perspectives of culture, I want to explore where culture comes from.

I have spent the better part of my entire professional life researching, both in applied and experimental settings, the concept of culture and how it is created and sustained. Essentially, my research in this area has uncovered three major areas that determine team culture:

» **Context:** The context refers to a number of elements. First, the *larger organizational culture* in which the team operates impacts the team culture, just as the national weather season impacts local weather forecasts. Second, the general dynamic of *expanding versus contracting* is a crucial contextual element that determines culture. Years ago, when I was working internally with EnPro Inc., the oil and gas markets turned south. When that happened, the expanding context that was fueling our growth (and our travel) turned and began to contract. Subsequently, hiring was put on hold, expenses were carefully scrutinized, and travel was suspended. That basic element—are we growing (expanding) or are we shrinking (contracting)—has a direct impact on team culture. Finally, the *history of the team*, including traditions, accomplishments, and failures, helps to create culture. Often, a new leader for a team fails to recognize their collective history, and the style and approach of a previous leader (or leaders). Allowing team members to discuss their history, and to provide their unique perspectives, is a powerful tool that can help a team make amends with the past and free the group to focus on the present and the future.

» **Individual members:** The styles of the individual team members (i.e., *achiever, affirmer,* and *asserter*) and the unique composition of those styles have an important role to play in creating team culture. The free assessment offered at the beginning of the book (http://www.atpfree.com) is designed to help team members understand the impact that their individual style has on the larger collective culture. Often thought of as something "out there," this book is designed to help each of us reconsider what impact our own style has on creating and sustaining team culture, for good or for ill.

» **The leader:** Finally, and perhaps most importantly, the style and shadow of the leader has a critical impact on the culture of a team or group. In fact, my research supports the notion that of all the other elements in play, the leader's style is the most important element in creating team culture. And therein lies a profound and sometimes uncomfortable truth for many managers and leaders: the team's culture that is creating so much frustration (e.g., "why can't they think for themselves!" "what happened to their creativity?" "why can't they bring solutions instead of just problems?" etc.) is often a result of the leader's style and shadow. In my TED Talk "The Power of Self Awareness," I go to great lengths to discuss the dysfunction in my failed marriage and the role that my need to be in control and to always be right played in creating dependency. Essentially, you can't have a co-dependent without a pro-dependent (an asserter in my framework), and that's where true self-discovery and self-awareness must start. To be more direct, the less-than-optimal culture of the team you are leading is likely a result of your dysfunction, just like my failed marriage was a result of mine. As such, I would encourage you to own and acknowledge your part in creating and sustaining your current team's culture, and to use this deep and powerful lever for real change and improvement.

The Psychodynamic Perspective of Team Culture

There are numerous frameworks or lenses to view small group behavior and team dynamics. From my perspective, the psychodynamic lens is not only the most valid, it also possesses the greatest utility in creating lasting, positive change in organizations. As Kurt Lewin famously said, "There is nothing more practical than a good theory." Or, as my former professor and advocate (and dear mentor and friend) at George Washington University Dr. John Lobuts said, "If you're going to go out on a theoretical limb, make sure you're standing on a sturdy branch." As previously stated, a psychodynamic perspective focuses on the impact that the unconscious has on human behavior, and I have found it to be the most practical and sturdy of all frameworks for understanding and predicting behavior.

In the broadest sense, the psychodynamic approach for understanding group behavior can be classified into two categories: psychoanalytic and humanistic (McLeod and Kettner-Polley 2004). The psychoanalytic approach falls under the *medical* metaphor, with an emphasis on diagnosis and description. In this camp, the works of Sigmund Freud, Wilfred Bion, and Carl Jung are paramount. The humanistic approach falls under the *developmental* metaphor, with an emphasis on learning and prescription. In this camp, the works of Kurt Lewin, Abraham Maslow, and again Carl Jung, are the most influential. The *Actualized Teamwork Framework* is my effort to synthesize both the psychoanalytical and humanistic approaches, taking the best from each, in order to create a valid and reliable model for both diagnosis (psychoanalytic) and development (humanistic).

Any discussion of psychodynamic theories must start with the founder of psychoanalysis, Sigmund Freud. Although Freud is most famous for his conception of the id, the ego, and the superego, he actually studied group behavior early in his career. Freud (1950) viewed groups as primitive collectivities grounded in extreme and irrational emotions that are unable to hold two competing ideas at the same time. Given this limited ability to appreciate ambiguity or the grey area that is very much a part of the human experience, especially in organizational life, groups are capable of only two emotions: love (often without measure) and hate (often without reason). His distinction between the id and the ego would greatly influence Wilfred Bion's work in group behavior, discussed in more detail shortly. One of Freud's famous students and later a well-known clinician and writer in her own right, Melanie Klein, expanded Freud's work in groups to help explain how the mature and conscious ego, when manifested at the group level, corresponds to reality-seeking behaviors and rational problem solving. Likewise, when the id manifests at the group level, neurotic behaviors and psychological regression, including projection and repression, emerge as protective mechanisms for the group.

The Swiss psychologist Carl Jung also explored group level behavior. Like Freud, he was convinced that groups existed, psychologically at least, to avoid reality and sustain their existence on illusions. In fact, Jung (2011) famously said that when "one hundred clever heads join together in a group, one big nincompoop is the result." That's about as blunt as you can get. At a much broader level, Jung was enamored by the notion of the *collective shadow*, which would include not only a team and organization, but in fact entire regions, nations, and ultimately, all of humanity (1912). Irrespective of the focus being on the individual or the group, Freud and Jung were united in the finding that confrontation—awareness, acknowledgement, and integration—was crucial if individuals and teams were going to realize their highest potential.

This brings us to Wilfred Bion, arguably the most influential thinker, researcher, and writer in small group behavior and the concept of team culture. Not only did Bion agree with Freud and Jung that the unconscious was a crucial part of group life, he was also able to classify and categorize the collective shadow found in groups. Bion referred to these shadow states as *basic assumption mental states*, or BAMS, and classified them into three major patterns of behavior: fight/flight, pairing, and dependency. In addition to the

BAMS, Bion (1961) identified the rational, conscious, and mature elements of team culture which he referred to as the *work group* (see Table 2.1).

Table 2.1. Unconscious and conscious elements of team culture

Unconscious		
BAMS	**ATP Culture**	**Emotion**
Fight/Flight	Detached	Anger and apathy
Pairing	Dramatic	Hope and frustration
Dependency	Dependent	Fear and anxiety
Conscious		
Work Group	**ATP Culture**	**Emotion**
	Dynamic	Passion and persistence

Bion (1961) found that team culture represents the "unanimous expression of the will of the group," and that there is no way an individual can do nothing in a group, "not even by doing nothing." He also found that of all the emotions we experience in groups, frustration is the most common. He believed that all behavior was group behavior, because even the hermit or recluse living alone was doing so with a reference to a larger collective which they wanted to avoid.

So, like me, you may be wondering where is the good news in group behavior and team culture? Is there any? The answer, according to Bion, is a resounding yes! Later in his career, Bion stated that "I attribute great force and influence to the work group...despite the basic assumptions, and sometimes in harmony with them, it is the work group that triumphs in the long run." He also stated belonging to and participating in group life was part of what makes us uniquely human, stating that "group life is essential to the full life of the individual" (1961).

Bion's influence has been significant and far-reaching. The well-known European writer and researcher Kets de Vries discusses collective mental activity that occurs in all groups and teams in formal settings, which leads to common perceptions and shared fantasies.

These fantasies, which are held as basic assumptions, shape the culture of the team.

Perhaps Bion's most important influence can be found in the literature related to group development theories. In the 1950s, Warren G. Bennis, Herbert A. Shepard, Dorothy Stock, and Herb Thelen all published theories of group development that were linear and sequential in nature (like personality development of the individual). Each proposed theory of group development contained the basic categories of the BAMS and the work group. Perhaps the most well-known theory of group development—*Forming, Storming, Norming and Performing*—was published by Bruce Tuckman in 1965. Originally known as Tuckman's Sequence, this theory has been adopted almost universally and is ubiquitous in most management and organizational psychology textbooks. And like the others before him, Tuckman used each of Bion's BAMS and his concept of the work group (i.e., performing) to create his model. However, Bion did not ever propose a model of linear, sequential group development. His model of group culture is much more dynamic, and because of the various elements that contribute to team culture (i.e., the context, individual members' styles, the leader's style and shadow), I believe that a nonlinear, non-sequential framework is much more valid and much more useful. The *Actualized Teamwork Framework* accounts for Bionic theory in this sense and does assume that one stage of development (i.e., culture) must be experienced before the next one can emerge. In fact, a change in the context, individual members and especially leadership can have profound impacts on culture, both positive and negative. I have personally facilitated and researched groups and teams that have experienced these kinds of profound improvements in culture where a Bionic, non-linear, and non-sequential model captures the essence of team culture and group life.

There are also three distinct leadership styles based on the dominant motive need of the leader: *achiever* (achievement need), *affirmer* (affiliation need), and the *asserter* (power need). The degree of self-actualization in each case dramatically impacts the team member engagement and performance. From a team effectiveness perspective, it is critical to remember that each leadership style and corresponding shadow helps create and foster a unique team culture. When the team leader is lacking in self-actualization, the resulting impact will create less than optimal cultures that impact communication, problem solving, decision making, and ultimately, team engagement.

Before we begin this discussion, a definition is in order. We are using *team* and *group* interchangeably in this chapter and define them as *three or more people who share a common goal.* Physical proximity is not necessary in order to meet this definition of a group or team. For example, ten strangers on an elevator going to work at different companies on different floors may share a very close physical proximity, but they do not share a common goal (unless the elevator becomes stuck between floors). Likewise, team members may spend very little time physically together, but because they share a common goal, language, and affiliation, they meet the definition of a group and, as such, are subject to the principles of small group behavior.

The four approaches to leader style in the Actualized Leadership Profile (ALP) Framework can be plotted on two dimensions: *orientation* and *problem-solving.* Orientation refers to mindset and focus of the leader. The ALP Framework illustrates task orientation based on the underlying motive need driving the leader's style. There are two distinct approaches that emerge: *tactical* and *strategic.* A more tactical orientation is a short-term, execution-focused approach that may be best described as rational, pragmatic, tangible, planned, practical, and cautious. The *achiever* and *affirmer* styles are more tactical. A more strategic orientation is a long-term, results-focused approach that may be best described as big picture, holistic, imaginative, spontaneous, objective, and risky. The *asserter* and *actualized* styles are more strategic.

The second dimension is based on problem-solving and decision-making. There are two basic approaches that emerge: *logical* and *intuitive*. A more logical approach to problem solving favors rationality, data, predictability, sensibility, process, and procedure. The *achiever* and *asserter* styles are more logical. A more intuitive approach to problem solving favors inference, novelty, gut feel, sixth sense, imagination, and play. The *affirmer* and *actualized* styles are more intuitive. Figure 2.2 provides a summary overview of the four approaches to leadership plotted on the two dimensions of orientation and problem-solving, yielding a 2×2 matrix.

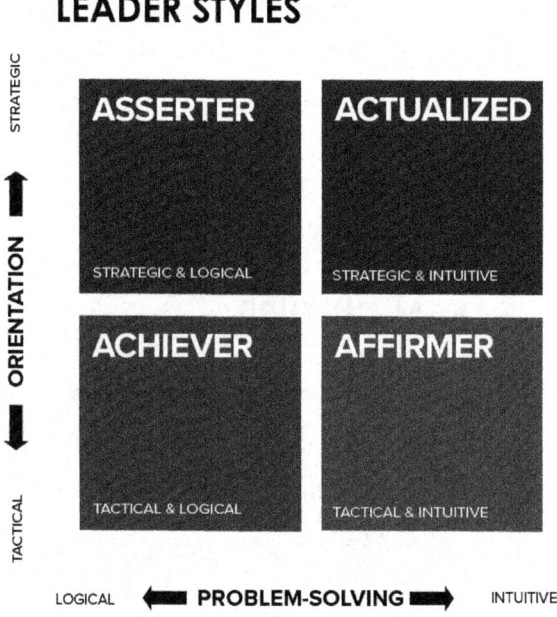

Figure 2.2. Leader style matrix

Research demonstrates the significant impact that leader style has on team culture and performance (Sparks, Pieri, and Kruger 2023.) As previously stated, culture is created and sustained from three primary forces: the leader's style and shadow, the styles of the individual members, and the broader context in which the team is operating. Of these three, our research strongly suggests that the leader has the greatest impact—for good or for ill—on their team's culture and performance.

Similar to the leadership styles, another **2×2** matrix for team culture can be created (see Figure 2.3). But, more importantly, it can also be mapped onto Figure 2.2 as an extension of leader style. As such, you can visually see what I refer to as the actualized performance cube (APC) (see Figure 2.4), which illustrates the connection between leader style and culture.

The team culture matrix is based on two dimensions: *performance and results* and *people and relationships. Performance and results* refers to the overall effectiveness of the team in accomplishing goals and productivity, classified as either *low* or *high*. The *detached* and *dramatic* cultures tend to perform at lower levels, while the *dependent* and *dynamic* cultures tend to perform at higher levels.

The second dimension is *people and relationships* and this refers to the overall engagement and connection that team members

TEAM CULTURE

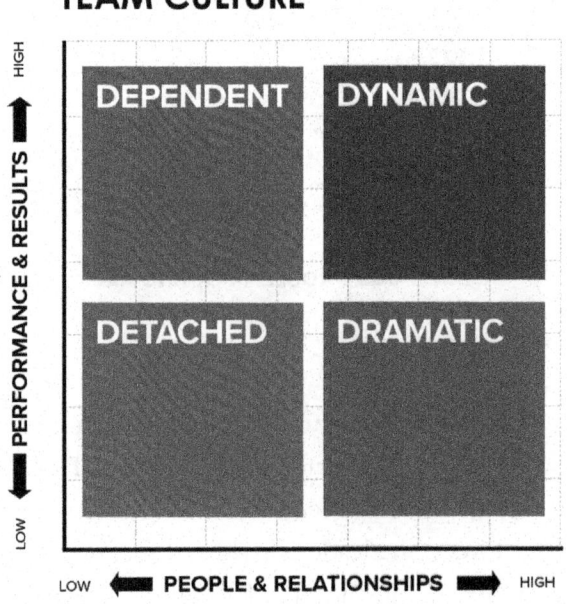

Figure 2.3. Team culture matrix

experience intrinsically, also classified as either *low* or *high*. The *detached* and *dependent* cultures are cooler and tend to have members that are less engaged and satisfied. The *dramatic* and *dynamic* cultures are warmer and tend to have members that are more engaged and satisfied.

Figure 2.3 illustrates the 2×2 matrix of team culture, and Figure 2.4 combines both the leader and team matrices to create the actualized performance cube (APC).

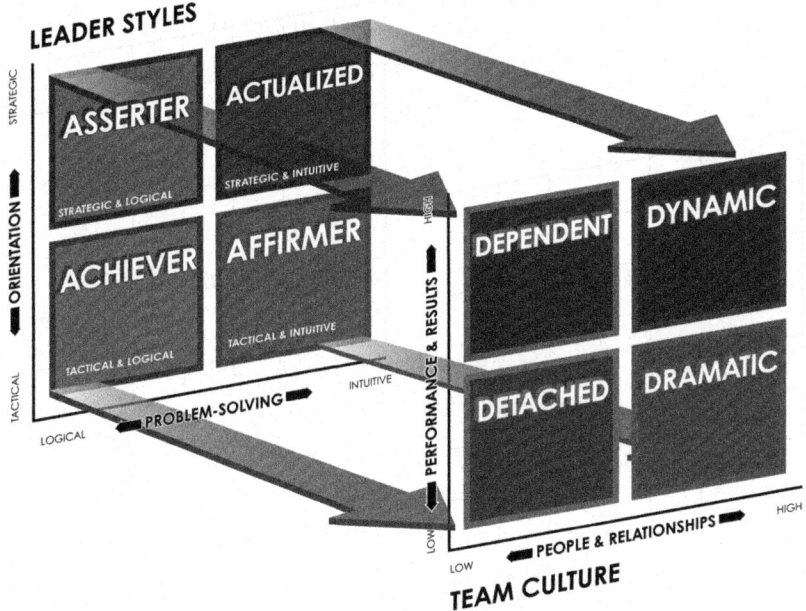

Figure 2.4. Actualized performance cube

The *Detached* Culture and the *Achiever* Style

A sad and paradoxical irony in life is that individuals who have a very high need for achievement, *achievers*, create the lowest performing culture in their teams, *detached*. Because of their need for absolute perfection, achievers sweat every detail while micromanaging their teams. Achievers are often too bogged down in the details and attempt to not only manage but often micromanage the business.

This culture is grounded in emotions of anger and apathy, and the resulting impact on the team from a group dynamics perspective is detachment. Team members express anger either aggressively, with open conflict and personal attacks, or passively by disengaging psychologically or physically. Psychological disengagement manifests when members become more interested in their mobile phones, iPads, or laptops than the meeting. Physical disengagement occurs when members habitually arrive late, leave early, or miss meetings altogether. Whether the anger is expressed actively or passively, members in a detached culture are not in the optimal position for candid discussions, healthy debate, and rational decision making. The most likely group decision-making pitfall facing this team culture is groupthink, which will be discussed in the next chapter.

The *Dramatic* Culture and the *Affirmer* Style

Now, imagine the extreme opposite end of the cool detachment spectrum from a detached culture and replace anger with kindness, rudeness with politeness, and despair with warmth and hope. At first this kind of team culture might sound more appealing, but it often results in the same degree of poor decision making and member disengagement. The *dramatic* culture is created and sustained by leaders who are primarily motivated out of the need for affiliation, *affirmers*, who focus on maintaining warm, harmonious, interpersonal relationships. These leaders want and need to be accepted and approved by their team at all costs. To this end, the team norm is one of politeness and friendliness to the extreme. Difficult or uncomfortable discussions are avoided or tabled for offline conversations that rarely occur. Although warm and personally supportive, the dramatic culture lacks collegial candor and frankness. Members often self-censor to avoid breaking the group norm of politeness and agreement. This culture is grounded in the emotion of frustration. Team members are friendly and polite on the surface, but this norm for niceness supersedes the need for healthy debate and conflict. Because candor and conflict are often avoided, members often leave meetings feeling frustrated and exasperated with the lack of progress or action. The most common group decision-making pitfall with the dramatic culture is the Abilene paradox, which will be discussed in the following chapter.

The *Dependent* Culture and the *Asserter* Style

It stands to reason that the majority of business leaders have a high need for power and independence, and thus exhibit the *asserter* leadership style. The resulting culture that emerges and is sustained by this style is *dependent*. My twenty-five-plus years of research consistently shows that this is the most common culture in Corporate America—whether Fortune 500 companies, non-profit organizations, or family units. The dependent culture is grounded in fear and anxiety with its default setting being *caution*. The asserter style is results-oriented and effective in the short-term, especially during a crisis. However, this style and the fear that it brings is not sustainable, and the long-term impact is quite dysfunctional. In a dependent culture, members look to their powerful leader for assurance, relying too heavily on their previous track record of accomplishments. Under stress, this leadership style can be dominating and autocratic, often shutting down attempts at open communication when it is needed most. Although these leaders are often extremely candid and blunt, they do not appreciate or tolerate any dissension. Members hesitate to speak out or challenge the leader, which often leads to poor decision-making. This culture is often difficult to identify because asserters are very adept at managing up, thus often enjoying a favorable impression from their manager. The norm of this culture is to follow the leader, and, as a result, the dependent culture often leads to either groupthink or the Abilene paradox when it comes to team decision-making.

The short descriptions presented above provide the basic categorical elements of the *Actualized Teamwork Framework*. Part 4 of the book examines in detail the elements of a more team-actualizing or dynamic culture, and the impact that individual self-actualization has on team culture and performance. Part 2 of the book will move into more detailed discussions and descriptions of each culture and will include applied examples from my consulting work over the years to illustrate both the behaviors of each culture and the collective shadow and unconscious emotionality that underlie each dynamic.

What's Next

Chapter 3 provides a detailed description and discussion of the detached culture. The chapter begins with an actual applied case study intended to help illustrate the behavioral and emotional dynamics of this culture, as well as an exploration of the achiever leadership style and the impact that micromanaging and perfectionism—at the expense of development and creativity—have on creating and sustaining the lowest performing culture.

PART II

LEADER AND
TEAM DYNAMICS

Chapter 3

The Detached Culture

What's in this chapter?

» The Detached Culture in Action
» Detached Culture Benchmark Code: Less Than or Equal to 20 Percent
» Characteristics of the Detached Culture
» The Leader and Team Shadow Cycle
» What's Next

Credit and blame smell the same.

—Dominic J. Monetta

THE BIG IDEA

Detached teams are usually an extension of an achiever leader. Their performance is low and the quality of their interpersonal relationships is poor. Detached teams have a collective shadow grounded in anger and apathy. Micromanaging tendencies from the leader create disengaged members who lack a common purpose or desire to work together. The desired score on the *detached* scale on the actualized team profile (ATP) is less than or equal to 20 percent.

Each of the leadership styles, *achiever, affirmer,* and *asserter,* has its own strengths that can lead to effectiveness and success in the workplace and in interpersonal relationships. But each style also has a *leadership shadow* that can become a career-limiting derailer when not effectively managed. Moreover, leadership shadows have a tremendous impact on creating and sustaining team culture. As discussed in Chapter 2, team culture directly impacts team decision making and problem solving, member engagement, and ultimately, performance. In this chapter, we examine the *detached culture* style and its connection to the achiever style and the *fear of failure leadership shadow.**

The Detached Culture in Action

An engineer by training, Fred was meticulous in everything he did. From his diet and exercise regimen, which he followed religiously, to his detail-orientation on every project he was assigned, he excelled in execution and delivering results.

In fact, Fred was so successful that he was promoted several times into increasingly responsible positions of leadership until he became a general manager/vice president and rumored heir apparent to the chief operations officer (COO). Fred's stock was at an all-time high except in one arena: his team of direct reports. As Fred's wins mounted and his reputation for execution grew, so did his number of direct reports. At the time I began working with him as an executive coach and consultant he had twelve direct reports of highly competent professionals. There was only one problem: Fred.

We started our engagement with a 360-degree assessment which produced very consistent, and very unflattering, feedback. Words and phrases in his feedback included "micromanager," "rigid and controlling," "workaholic," and "overbearing." Fred's initial reaction

---

* In chapters 3, 4, and 5, the names for the "culture in action" sections have been modified for privacy. The details and descriptions have not.

was very predictable—deflection. After carefully dissecting the content and word choices of the qualitative (open-ended) responses provided, he was fairly certain he knew who said what. I reminded him several times that was irrelevant, but I got the very strong suspicion that it mattered very much to him. He then attempted to deflect the feedback by commenting on their jealousy and envy. Fred was actually one of the younger members of his team, and his tenure with the company was also shorter than his average direct report's. As such, he surmised that the feedback was based on jealousy at his rapid ascent in the organization.

But the cracks in his team's armor were starting to show. While he had been in the role for just over six months, the team had not yet gelled. In fact, the chief executive officer (CEO) shared with me that he was of the opinion that they were "moving in the wrong direction." The results of their Actualized Team Profile (ATP) clearly showed a detached culture in the *intense range* (see Figure 3.1). Members were somewhere on the continuum between anger and apathy, with several telling me, "Why bother, he's going to redo my work anyway."

As I prepared for our teambuilding session, I met with Fred to review his goals and objectives and, in what I found to be a rare moment of personal reflection, he made a comment about

ASSERTER Strategic and Logical	ACTUALIZED Strategic and Intuitive
DEPENDENT High Performance & Results, Low People & Relationship	DYNAMIC High Performance & Results, High People & Relationship
ACHIEVER Tactical and Logical	AFFIRMER Tactical and Intuitive
DETACHED Low Performance & Results, Low People & Relationship	DRAMATIC Low Performance & Results, High People & Relationship

Figure 3.1. Detached culture team profile

> **DETACHED CULTURE EXAMPLE**
>
> **BAMS and underlying emotionality**: Fight/flight; Anger and apathy
>
> **Patterns of behavior**: Disagreement, open conflict, disengagement, tardiness, and withdrawal
>
> **Norms**: Interrupting and talking over others, being distracted and challenging each other at every turn, arriving late, leaving early, and oscillating between heated exchanges and total resignation
>
> **Leadership style**: Achiever and the fear of failure leadership shadow
>
> **Eternal question**: Am I worthy?

his childhood. He was the younger brother and admitted that he felt like he never really measured up to his older brother who was extremely successful in his own right. The older brother, let's call him Steve, had attended a private university on an athletic scholarship. He graduated with honors, earned an Master of Business Administration (MBA) from a Top 10 program, and started his own business. He had recently cashed out and sold the business for millions, much to his father's pride and delight. Fred, on the other hand, had attended a public university on a partial academic scholarship. He took out student loans to make up the difference. He had also earned an MBA at night, but from a much lesser known and respected program. He was always comparing himself to his brother. And here's the irony—while Fred was extremely accomplished and successful in his own right, he always felt less-than and inadequate when he compared himself to his brother. And it appeared that his father helped to perpetuate this competition. No matter what Fred did, he didn't feel like it was enough. So his eternal question—*Am I worthy?*—constantly played in the recesses of his psyche. And as we've discussed both in this book and in *Actualized Leadership: Meeting Your Shadow & Maximizing Your Potential*, the self-fulfilling nature of paradoxical intent was starting to play out in his team dynamics. Fred had created a *detached* culture and if that pattern was not broken, the last stop on this train ride would be failure.

Characteristics of the Detached Culture

The Detached Culture: Achiever Leadership Style

Achievers often create the lowest performing culture, detached. Because of their need for absolute perfection, achievers sweat every detail while micromanaging their teams. A detached culture is grounded in emotions of anger and apathy, and the resulting impact on the team from a group dynamics perspective is detachment. Members express anger either aggressively, with open conflict and personal attacks, or passively by disengaging psychologically or physically. Psychological disengagement manifests when members become more interested in their mobile phones, iPads, or laptops than the meeting. Physical disengagement occurs when members habitually arrive late, leave early, or miss meetings altogether. Whether the anger is expressed actively or passively, members in a detached culture are not in the optimal position for candid discussions, healthy debate, and rational decision-making. The most likely group decision-making pitfall facing this team culture is groupthink, which is discussed in Chapter 6.

The Leader and Detached Team Shadow Cycle

Achievers are the performance backbone of organizations. Their high need for achievement instills a drive for winning, success, improvement, and accomplishment. They are excellent accountants, planners, organizers, and salespeople and they often strike out on their own for entrepreneurial success.

Achievers present as competent, efficient, detail-oriented and together, and they have a competitive, high-energy can-do attitude. They tend to have a bias toward action, converting ideas into projects with little or no lag time; as pragmatic bottom-liners, they focus on seeing those projects through to completion.

Their ambition to be the best they can be, however, can lead achievers to get bogged down in details, micromanage their teams, and to identify with work alone. This inattention to the human side may leave coworkers feeling used and devalued (see Figure 3.2).

Today there is a resounding interest in inclusive leadership, which is very similar to the employee involvement movement that was coupled with Total Quality Management (TQM) in the 1980s and 1990s. The difference between inclusive leadership and employee involvement is the explicit focus on leader behaviors and the common barriers, or what I refer to as *microtransgressions*, that leaders create and, while subtle, can stifle team member engagement and input. My research has focused on linking unique patterns of bias and microtransgressions to the unique leadership shadows.

Shadow bias, more commonly referred to as unconscious bias, refers to implicit or underlying biases that reside in our subconscious and very often impact our behavior without our conscious awareness. For the achiever style, there are two primary patterns that need

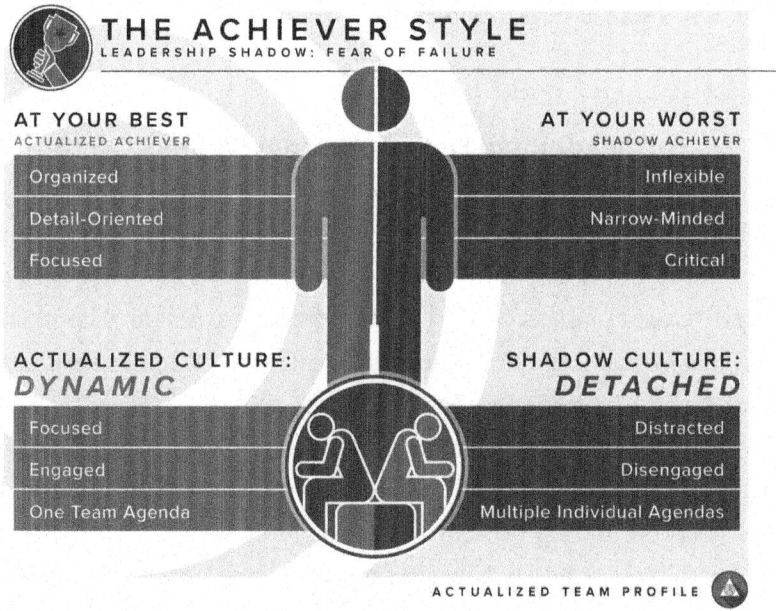

Figure 3.2. The achiever style

to be recognized: *affinity bias* and the *horn effect*. Figure 3.3 presents the achiever and fear of failure shadow bias cycle.

Shadow Bias

Affinity bias is the tendency to have a preference for, or an affinity for, others that are very similar to you. For example, you may prefer working with other people who look like you, attended your same alma mater, or have similar life experience (e.g., first generation college graduate, raised in a certain part of the country, etc.). For many achievers, this bias plays out with a preference for coworkers who are just as organized as you. Maybe their to-do lists are color-coded like yours, or perhaps they use spreadsheets to track progress like you do.

The reason affinity bias is a concern is because you may be discounting the input and creativity of your team members who are different. Maybe a team member who is an affirmer and more relationship-oriented or an asserter, whose moments of insight into a complex problem or bold and decisive action occur outside of an agreed upon process or fall outside of strict policy. As an achiever, being more mindful of your tendency to discount others because of their differences can help enable you to consider and value the involvement and input of every member of your team and, in doing so, become a more inclusive leader.

The *horn effect* is the exact opposite of its more well-known sister, the *halo effect* (discussed in the next chapter). This bias occurs when you allow one negative aspect of an individual's performance

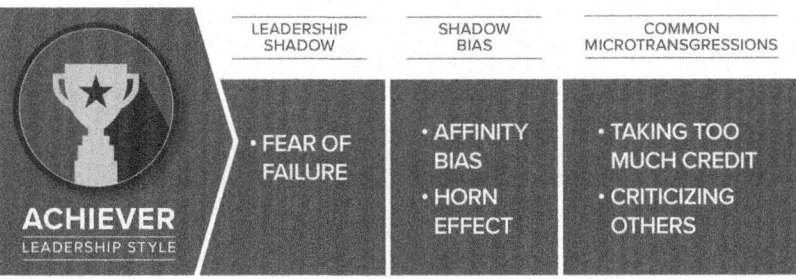

LEADERSHIP SHADOW	SHADOW BIAS	COMMON MICROTRANSGRESSIONS
• FEAR OF FAILURE	• AFFINITY BIAS • HORN EFFECT	• TAKING TOO MUCH CREDIT • CRITICIZING OTHERS

ACHIEVER LEADERSHIP STYLE

Figure 3.3. The achiever and fear of failure shadow bias cycle

to cloud your judgment and objective appraisal of their entire effort. This is linked to the shadow tendency of many achievers to be critical. As discussed in my book *Actualized Leadership*, very often achievers are extremely critical and hard on themselves, and they often project this negativity onto others. It is important to stay objective and navigate the ambiguous and grey waters of human behavior and performance, and to provide feedback accordingly. This also occurs when a past mistake of a direct report stays in the back of your mind and adversely influences your interactions with them. It's important to move forward and approach your interactions, and especially your feedback, with an open and objective mindset.

Microtransgressions

Common microtransgressions of the achiever style, which in this case are more commonly referred to as microaggressions, include taking too much credit and criticizing others. Achievers have such a strong need for, well, achievement and success that they sometimes can't help themselves from taking too much credit. But we would be well-advised to remember the wise adage my late mentor Dr. Dominic J. Monetta taught me: "credit and blame smell the same." In other words, be careful when you raise your hand to take more than your fair share of the credit when a solution or project appears to be very positive. As we all know, what looks great today can sour quickly, and when that same project gets sideways in the future, your hand that was raised for the credit must stay up for the blame. Many achievers attempt to lower said hand into a pointed finger when things do go off the rails and point to the culprit who is to blame. And that is related to the second microtransgression, criticizing others. Senior leaders and C-suite executives time and again tell me how much they are impressed when an individual takes the blame for something, as opposed to blaming and criticizing others. Taking responsibility quickly allows for a faster remedy and pivot to resolution. Actualized achievers are much more likely to take responsibility, what Jim Collins in *Good to Great* referred to as "looking in the mirror" when things do go poorly, and, in doing so, build more trust and create greater engagement for their teammates.

Leadership Shadow: Fear of Failure

Experiencing stress in the form of ambiguity or losing triggers the fear of failure leadership shadow in achievers; when that happens, the negative traits cited previously emerge. Under stress, an achiever will transform in unproductive ways: organized becomes rigid, detail-oriented devolves to being obsessive, and expertise leads to micro-management. The irony is that this fear of failure leadership shadow makes achievers more likely to fail.

As stated in Chapter 3, the leadership shadow cycle starts with irrational thoughts, which create unfounded feelings, which in turn lead to counterproductive and self-defeating—or shadow—behaviors, as illustrated in Figure 3.4.

You might be asking yourself how, exactly, could this be? Wouldn't fearing failure actually help prevent it? To a certain degree, a healthy fear of failure can lead to new levels of achievement, such as getting up earlier, working later, or striving to achieve your goals. However, if left unabated and unmanaged, this cycle will eventually lead achievers to the one place they fear the most: failure.

What's Next

Chapter 4 provides a detailed description and discussion of the *dramatic* culture. The chapter begins with an actual applied case study intended to help illustrate the behavioral and emotional dynamics of this culture, as well as an exploration of the *affirmer* leadership style and the impact that avoiding conflict and being overly accommodating—at the expense of candid feedback and focus on execution—has on creating and sustaining the low performing culture that results in feelings of frustration and despair for team members.

Irrational Thoughts	Unfounded Feelings	Self-Defeating Behaviors
I always have to be perfect	Frustration	Becoming obsessive and nitpicky
No one else can do this as well as I can	Critical	Being overly critical and micromanaging
I am not enough	Inadequate	Taking on too many projects, or staying over-scheduled

⇩

Unconscious Desire for Success and Admiration

⇩

Leadership Trap: Micromanager

⇩

Basic Assumptions	Group Emotions	Team Behaviors
Fight/Flight We must fight or retreat The enemy is out there	Anger and apathy	Open hostility and conflict Disengaged and distracted Multiple competing agendas Evasive and vague input Delay making decisions

⇩

Results: Failure and Resentment

Figure 3.4. The leadership shadow cycle: Achiever

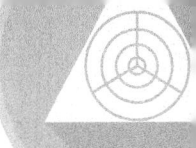

Chapter 4

The Dramatic Culture

What's in this chapter?

» The Dramatic Culture in Action
» The Dramatic Culture Code Benchmark: Less Than or Equal to 30 Percent
» Characteristics of the Dramatic Culture
» The Leader and Team Shadow Cycle
» What's Next

> *We don't fear the unknown. We fear separation.*
>
> —Jerry B. Harvey

THE BIG IDEA

Dramatic teams are usually an extension of an affirmer leadership style. Their performance is low but the quality of their interpersonal relationships is warm and friendly. Dramatic teams have a collective shadow grounded in frustration and despair. Conflict-avoidance by the leader and emphasis on relationships instead of, or sometimes at the expense of, performance create frustrated members who lack candor and are often unrealistically optimistic for the future. The desired score on the Dramatic scale on the Actualized Team Profile (ATP) is less than or equal to 30 percent.

In the previous chapter we discussed the *achiever* style and the resulting *detached* culture. As discussed in Chapter 2, team culture directly impacts team decision making and problem solving, member engagement, and ultimately, performance. In this chapter, we examine the *dramatic* culture and its connection to the *affirmer* style and the *fear of rejection leadership shadow*.

The Dramatic Culture in Action

A nurse by training, Nancy had transitioned from healthcare into the non-profit world where she served as executive director for a large, well-known, and well-respected 501(c)(3) focused on healthcare access and equity. She was a people-person through and through, often taking time out of a very busy schedule to visit with both her clients and team members, discussing a wide range of challenges, both personal and professional. Everyone liked and trusted Nancy.

But not everyone respected Nancy as a leader. While it would be almost impossible not to appreciate her warm smile and generous spirit, her team of direct reports was growing increasingly frustrated at her unwillingness to call out low performers and her tolerance for some team members phoning it in. Nancy had started to sense that employee engagement, and perhaps even performance, were starting to lag.

The organization had a total of approximately fifty employees, with eight of them serving as direct reports to Nancy. Nancy, who lives and works in the midwestern United States, had reached out to me after viewing my TED Talk "The Power of Self Awareness" and was fascinated with Jerry Harvey and his concept of mismanaged agreement. We decided to assess the team and, as a part of our session, show the video "The Abilene Paradox."

After viewing "The Abilene Paradox" I turned off the smart TV screen and asked the question "So, are we on the road to Abilene?" like I had done so many times before. I was not fully prepared for the explosion of pent-up frustration and exasperation. As had been the case many times in the past, the video had effectively fulfilled its purpose of serving as an invitation to discuss the undiscussables, and to identify mismanaged agreement. One by one her direct reports lamented bad team decisions, poor performance being tolerated, and the multiple white elephants in the room that were draining the team, and the entire organization, of its vitality and energy. The norm of politeness had expired, and the resulting conversation was candid and very direct.

What I remember most about this experience was the team conveying and reinforcing their love for Nancy. There was no denying that she was a wonderful, thoughtful leader who cared deeply for her team and her organization's mission. But they were also extremely frustrated. The team needed her to make some tough decisions so that the entire organization could flourish and thrive. As Nancy took all this feedback to heart, I could see that she was feeling a lot of emotion. Confrontation with the shadow and recognition of paradoxical intent (the more you fear something the more likely you are to experience it) always produces this response. She began to realize the wisdom of what Jung, Frankl, Harvey, and others have been saying for a very long time. The very thing she was trying so hard to avoid—separation and rejection—were staring her in the face because of her unwillingness to meet conflict head-on, engage in difficult conversations, and provide direct performance feedback to the lower performers who appeared to be very much taking advantage of her warm and friendly affirmer disposition. Said another way, we meet our destiny on the road we take to avoid it. In Nancy's case, her destiny—rejection—was being confronted on the very road—avoiding conflict and sugar-coating the truth so as not to hurt anyone's feelings—she had been on to avoid it (see Figure 4.1).

Nancy had grown up in a household where both parents were high-functioning alcoholics. Moreover, she was the middle daughter, having both an older and a younger sister. It is not uncommon for a child growing up in this dynamic to take on the

ASSERTER Strategic and Logical **DEPENDENT** High Performance & Results, Low People & Relationship	**ACTUALIZED** Strategic and Intuitive **DYNAMIC** High Performance & Results, High People & Relationship
ACHIEVER Tactical and Logical **DETACHED** Low Performance & Results, Low People & Relationship	**AFFIRMER** Tactical and Intuitive **DRAMATIC** Low Performance & Results, High People & Relationship

Figure 4.1. Dramatic culture team profile

DRAMATIC CULTURE EXAMPLE

BAMS and underlying emotionality: Pairing; Frustration and despair

Patterns of behavior: Polite conversation, self-censoring, consensus-building, conflict avoidance and unrealistic hope for future salvation

Norms: Warm, friendly, supportive, and polite climate that supports the individual members, future-oriented with hopeful expectation, failure to enforce performance standards or address low performers, growing despair and exasperation at the lack of authenticity and candor in the meetings

Leadership style: Affirmer and the fear of rejection leadership shadow

Eternal question: Am I wanted?

---

peacemaker role. She experienced volatility at times with her parents, especially her father. As such, she remembered growing up feeling like she was walking on eggshells so as not to rock the boat. Additionally, as the middle child, she felt like she was always brokering the peace between her sisters, or one sister and a parent. Her needs and wants took a back seat to the needs and wants of her other family members, and this pattern had played out in both her professional life (dramatic team culture) and her personal life (divorced from her spouse after looking the other way for years).

From as early as she could remember, she had avoided conflict and tried to always look on the positive side, even if it meant denying reality. So her eternal question—*Am I wanted?*—constantly played in the recesses of her psyche. And as we've discussed both in this book and in *Actualized Leadership: Meeting Your Shadow & Maximizing Your Potential,* the self-fulfilling nature of paradoxical intent was starting to play out in her team dynamics. Nancy had created a dramatic culture and if that pattern was not broken, the last stop on this train would be separation and rejection.

Characteristics of the Dramatic culture

The Dramatic Culture: Affirmer Leadership Style

To fully appreciate how it feels to participate in a dramatic culture, it may be helpful to imagine the exact opposite of the *detached* culture and replace anger with kindness, rudeness with politeness, and despair with hope. At first this kind of team culture might sound more appealing, but it often results extreme feelings of frustration and the same degree of poor decision-making. The dramatic culture is created and sustained by leaders who are primarily motivated out of the need for affiliation, affirmers, who focus on maintaining warm, harmonious, interpersonal relationships. These leaders want and need to be accepted and approved by their team at all costs. To this end, the team norm is one of politeness and friendliness to the extreme. Difficult or uncomfortable discussions are avoided or tabled for offline conversations that rarely occur. Members often self-censor to avoid breaking the group norm of politeness and agreement. Team members are friendly and polite on the surface, but this norm for niceness supersedes the need for healthy debate and conflict. Because candor and conflict are often avoided, team members often leave meetings feeling frustrated and exasperated with the lack of progress or action. The most common group decision-making pitfall with the dramatic culture is the Abilene paradox, which will be discussed in the following chapter.

The previous chapter addressed the *achiever* leadership style, which is characterized by a strong drive for winning, success, and accomplishment. Under stress, however, achievers may be confronted by the fear of failure, the leadership shadow that undermines their strengths. In this chapter, we examine the *affirmer* style and its leadership shadow, fear of rejection.

The Leader and Dramatic Team Shadow Cycle

Affirmers are the social glue that connects and holds us together in our organizations. Affirmers are warm, friendly, loyal individuals who care deeply for others. With their strong need for affiliation, their primary motivation is to develop and maintain harmonious interpersonal relationships; they have an intrinsic need for connection with others and for love and acceptance.

As excellent connectors and team members, affirmers often work in human resources, counseling, social work, and teaching. Many famous affirmers, like Pope John Paul II, Mahatma Gandhi, and Mother Teresa, come from faith-based traditions. They are the best and most empathetic listeners in the world, always ready to hear about our latest triumph, tragedy, or challenge.

Their concern for people and relationships over performance and results, and their desire and need to be accepted and approved by the group at all costs, can often hinder their success. Affirmers strive to avoid conflict and difficult or uncomfortable discussions, and the result is often a lack of candor, authenticity, and productivity (see Figure 4.2).

From an inclusion perspective, the common barriers, or what I refer to as *microtransgressions*, that leaders create and sustain, while subtle, can frustrate member engagement and candid communication. My research has focused on linking unique patterns of bias and microtransgressions to the unique leadership shadows.

Shadow bias, more commonly referred to as unconscious bias, refers to implicit or underlying biases that reside in our subconscious and very often impact our behavior without our conscious awareness. For the affirmer style there are two primary patterns that need to be recognized: *conformity bias* and the *halo effect*. Figure 4.3 presents the affirmer and fear of rejection shadow bias cycle.

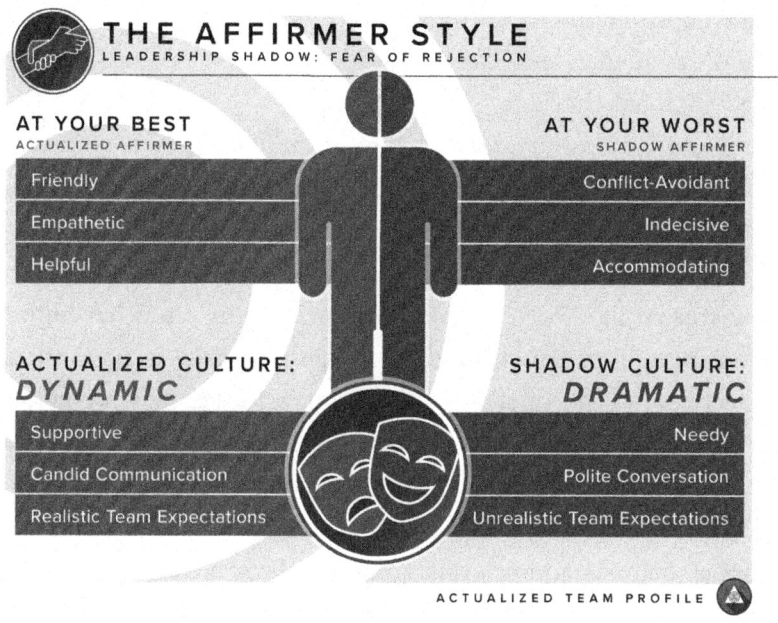

Figure 4.2. The affirmer style

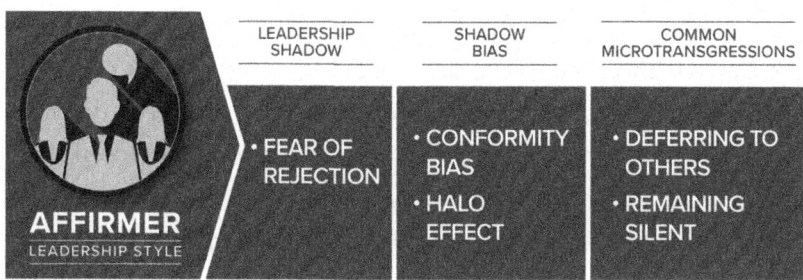

Figure 4.3. The affirmer and fear of rejection shadow bias cycle

Shadow Bias

Conformity bias is the tendency to conform your attitudes and behavior to the group norm. For example, you may adjust your opinion or perspective on a topic or issue based on the group's desire and attitude. This dynamic can be especially dysfunctional because taken to the extreme it represents the foundation for mob mentality. For example, an off-handed or inappropriate comment may be made about another individual. Affirmers are more likely to laugh that off as an innocent joke instead of taking a stand and calling out unacceptable behavior.

Freud famously said that groups experience only two emotions in the extreme: love and hate. For the dramatic culture, this dynamic always manifests as love and the reason this is dysfunctional is because the leader must be objective and comfortable in the ambiguity or grey area of life. For example, *dramatic* teams often have unrealistic expectations for the future. Something new—a new offering or service, new product, new market, new leader, new merger, and the like—will provide salvation for the team. *Actualized affirmers* have a heightened awareness for this tendency to emerge and move quickly to effectively manage expectations by engaging in more rational dialogue and painting a more realistic picture of the future. Without this awareness and action, the unrealistic and overly optimistic expectations begin to take on a life of their own, building off each other until a future scenario completely detached from reality sets in. And eventually when the team's expectations are not met, the warmth and hope of the group turn to frustration and despair.

The *halo effect* is the exact opposite of the *horn effect* (discussed in the last chapter). This bias occurs when you allow one positive aspect of an individual's performance to cloud your judgment and objectively appraise their entire effort across all job-related competencies. This is linked to the shadow tendency of many affirmers to be warm, friendly, and caring. As discussed in my book *Actualized Leadership*, very often affirmers are reluctant to give critical performance feedback to their direct reports, not wanting to rock the boat or upset the other individual. It is important to lead with objectivity and navigate the ambiguous and grey waters of human behavior and performance, and to provide fair and valid feedback accordingly.

Microtransgressions

Common microtransgressions of the affirmer style, which in this case are more commonly referred to as *microaffirmations*, include deferring to others and remaining silent, which often denotes approval and acceptance. Affirmers often rate their abilities and skills lower than their raters (e.g., a 360-degee assessment, etc.) and often discount their experience and intuition. As a result, they are more likely to defer to others, including direct reports. This is considered a microtransgression because very often affirmers are actually right and their voice should not only be heard, but also prevail. Related to deferring to others is the transgression or microaffirmation of remaining silent. This often occurs in two broad ways. First, affirmers may be silent when something inappropriate or offensive is said. Allowing something unacceptable to pass by is related to the sin of omission. Instead of committing an act against another person or party, the sin of omission is leaving something out or not taking an action. The second broad category is missing an opportunity to provide performance feedback to a team member by remaining silent to carefully think about exactly what you want to say and when you want to say it. While I certainly understand the desire to be thoughtful in the way you give feedback, it's been my experience that a silent pause often leads to no feedback being given for a variety of reasons, including "too much time has passed at this point." As such, actualized affirmers, while collaborative, are not shy about putting their opinion and perspective in the room. And, they rarely let an opportunity go by to give feedback to others or to address comments or perspectives that may exclude or offend others.

Leadership Shadow: Fear of Rejection

When conflict, confrontation, or the potential of a damaged or lost relationship is presented, the resulting stress triggers the fear of rejection leadership shadow in affirmers. Friendliness becomes conflict avoidance, concern for others leads to being overly accommodating, and differing opinions and perspectives create indecisiveness. Just as with achievers and their fear of failure, affirmers are more likely to feel what they fear most—rejection and separation—when their fear of rejection leadership shadow is activated.

The irrational thoughts, unfounded feelings, and self-defeating—or shadow—behaviors that affirmers display through their fear of rejection are illustrated in Figure 4.4.

When affirmers ignore their own needs, or the needs of the group, in an effort to be accepted and accommodating, the lack of candor and transparency can lead to poor decision making and discord. And the outcome that affirmers fear most—rejection—is often exactly what results. This rejection can be felt from direct reports or can tragically result in separation either from the team (e.g., demotion back to being an individual contributor, etc.) or being released from the organization.

What's Next

Chapter 5 provides a detailed description and discussion of the *dependent* culture. The chapter begins with an actual applied case study intended to help illustrate the behavioral and emotional dynamics of this culture, as well as an exploration of the *asserter* leadership style and the impact that being controlling and creating compliance and dependency—at the expense of creativity and healthy debate—has on creating and sustaining the low performing culture that results in feelings of fear and anxiety in team members.

Irrational Thoughts	Unfounded Feelings	Self-Defeating Behaviors
I cannot be alone	Insecure	Staying in unhealthy relationships
The needs of others are more important than my own	Insignificant	Ignoring your own needs and being overly accommodating
I should not anger others	Weak	Allowing others to take advantage of you

⇩

Unconscious Desire for Connection and Approval

⇩

Leadership Trap: Conflict-Avoider

⇩

Basic Assumptions	Group Emotions	Team Behaviors
Unrealistic hope for the future	Frustration and despair	Polite conversation over candor
Anticipation for salvation		Differences smoothed over
Personal social needs outweigh productive output		Avoid obvious problems
		Being accepted by the group
		Enthusiasm for the future

⇩

Results: Separation and Criticism

Figure 4.4. The leadership shadow cycle: Affirmer

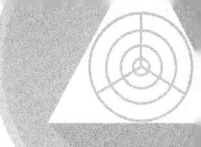

Chapter 5

The Dependent Culture

What's in this chapter?

» The Dependent Culture in Action
» The Dependent Culture Code Benchmark: Less Than or Equal to 40 Percent
» Characteristics of the Dependent culture
» The Leader and Team Shadow Cycle
» What's Next

When you try to control everything, you end up enjoying nothing.

—Anonymous

> **THE BIG IDEA**
>
> Dependent teams are usually an extension of an asserter leadership style. Their performance is moderate to high, but the quality of their interpersonal relationships is poor. Dependent teams have a collective shadow grounded in fear and anxiety. Controlling and autocratic behavior on the part of the leader that emphasizes loyalty and obedience, as opposed to mature debate and dialogue, creates a fear-based environment where team members are afraid to voice their true opinions and beliefs. The desired score on the Dependent scale on the actualized team profile (ATP) is less than or equal to 40 percent.

Like the other leadership styles, *achiever* and *affirmer*, the *asserter* style has valuable strengths that can be negated by its leadership shadow. Asserters are bold, strategic, and decisive, but their fear of betrayal can make them skeptical and controlling. They are driven out of a need for independence and freedom, and demand loyalty from others. However, their leadership shadow often brings about the exact opposite—betrayal and codependence—often found in the *dependent* culture.

The Dependent Culture in Action

Carlos seemed to almost be a force of nature. His work ethic was matched only by his unwavering belief in himself and his ability to accomplish anything he committed to. Raised by his mother, from an early age he learned to take charge of situations and internalized the wise adage "the Lord helps those who help themselves." He earned a doctorate in information technology (IT) and while he had planned to go into academia, there was just too much money in the private sector. He had worked at numerous companies and had recently been promoted to chief information officer (CIO) and clearly had his sights set on one other office—the CEO's. There was just one problem: Carlos' team. Carlos had been described as brash and arrogant, ruled with an iron fist, and demanded total loyalty from his direct reports. Formal and always impeccably dressed, he sat the head of the table for his meetings and everyone knew that Carlos would have the first, and last, word.

Lately, Carlos had begun to complain about the team regressing and his perception that no one could make a decision without him. As this dynamic became more apparent, he became more and more frustrated. He felt like he had to make all the decisions and come up with all the creative solutions to the many challenges and problems they faced daily. He was right in one regard. He was making or approving all decisions, and it was starting to wear him down. But he had not yet fully accepted that he had created this dependent environment and now, over time, had begun to resent it (see Figure 5.1).

I asked him if he would be willing to watch my TED Talk "The Power of Self Awareness," which is one part Chapter 1: "My F in Life," from *Actualized Leadership*, and one part tribute to the late, great Jerry Harvey. The next time we met, Carlos had a sort of distant, reluctant acceptance in his eyes. Before I could even sit down he blurted out, "So, I watched your TED Talk and I feel like you

ASSERTER Strategic and Logical **DEPENDENT** High Performance & Results, Low People & Relationship	ACTUALIZED Strategic and Intuitive **DYNAMIC** High Performance & Results, High People & Relationship
ACHIEVER Tactical and Logical **DETACHED** Low Performance & Results, Low People & Relationship	AFFIRMER Tactical and Intuitive **DRAMATIC** Low Performance & Results, High People & Relationship

Figure 5.1. Dependent culture team profile

DEPENDENT CULTURE EXAMPLE

BAMS and underlying emotionality: Dependency; Fear and anxiety

Patterns of behavior: Deferring to the leader, asking for assistance, keeping your head down, agreeing with the leader on every point, not challenging assumptions

Norms: Believing that the leader always knows best; using vague or cautious language to gauge sentiment; inherent belief in tradition, policies, and procedures to provide security and predictability; lack of candor and sincere communication

Leadership style: Asserter and the fear of betrayal leadership shadow

Eternal question: Am I safe?

are trying to tell me that the culture issue is my fault." I responded that I was not trying to tell him that, I was, in fact, telling him that. You can't have a dependent (e.g., spouse, friend, team, etc.) without a pro-dependent which is, essentially, another name for an asserter. Now in a deeper reflection, he said, "So in order to fix them, you've got to fix me first?" "No," I said, "I can't fix anyone but myself. You are the only one who can acknowledge, and integrate, *your* shadow." Hired as his executive coach and consultant, I was tasked with helping him soften his edges because turnover on his team was starting to add up. In fact, that was really the only place I could find developmental feedback for Carlos (other than the CEO and chief financial officer [CFO]). You see, his current direct reports were reluctant, if not outright scared, to say anything negative about Carlos.

Here is what I found extremely interesting. Carlos was very self-aware and reflective. He let me know that he had attended several leadership development programs and as for assessments, he had "taken them all." That included the Actualized Leader Profile (ALP) assessment, and his response to his ALP results (intense asserter), like so many asserters, was "Oh I knew that, doesn't surprise me at all!" (awkward laughter follows). But here's the thing: he really did know "that" (what I call an asserter and more specifically, the shadow tendencies of this style). He recognized the impact that his style and shadow had on others, both at the office and at home.

The challenge for asserters in general, and Carlos specifically, is trusting that a new approach will work. His success up to this point was undeniable, but like with the other styles, the cracks in the team were really starting to show. His reputation was taking a hit as direct reports ejected from his team (which he took very personally) and then felt secure enough to voice complaints. And therein lies the growth challenge for asserters: letting our guard down, embracing vulnerability, and allowing others to flourish around us all the while trusting the process of letting go. We were a long way from this point, however, as the results from his team's ATP showed an intensely *dependent* culture.

And even though he knew intellectually that he could trust his team and himself, he was having a very difficult time not stepping in and solving the team's problems, giving commands, and being right. So his eternal question—*Am I safe?*—constantly played in the recesses of his psyche. And as we've discussed both in this book and in *Actualized Leadership: Meeting Your Shadow & Maximizing Your Potential*, the self-fulfilling nature of paradoxical intent was starting to play out in his team dynamics. Carlos had created a dependent culture and the realization that the dependency that he was starting to resent was of his own doing was staring him directly in the face. As someone who applauded his unique ability to "confront reality and the often-brutal facts that lie beneath it" he was beginning to accept that his destiny—betrayal—was lurking around the corner.

Fast forward to our meeting day at a lavish hotel in Asheville, North Carolina. As we assembled around the hotel meeting space for our team development session, I could feel the tension and apprehension in the air. While the team had been reluctant to provide any constructive feedback to Carlos, there was no mistaking the team culture report and the dependent profile contained within. All eyes were on Carlos to see how he would respond.

Characteristics of the Dependent culture

The Dependent Culture: Asserter Leadership Style

My research over the last thirty years, both applied and anecdotal, demonstrates time and again that the most common style in the C-suite is an asserter with the resulting culture developed and sustained by this style being dependent. The dependent culture is grounded in fear and anxiety with its critical attribute being *caution*. As previously discussed, the asserter style is results-oriented and effective in the short-term, especially during a crisis. However, this style and the fear that it brings is not sustainable, and the long-term impact is quite dysfunctional. In a dependent culture, team members look to their powerful leader for assurance, relying too heavily on their previous track record of accomplishments. Under stress, this leadership style can be dominating and autocratic, often shutting down attempts at open communication when it is needed most. Although these leaders are often extremely candid and blunt, they do not appreciate or tolerate any dissension. It is critical to engage other members of their team to assess the impact of the leader's style on both the overall dynamic and culture of the group and on the organization as a whole. The norm of this culture is to follow the leader, and, as a result, the dependent culture often leads to either groupthink or the Abilene paradox when it comes to team decision making.

The Leader and Dependent Team Shadow Cycle

Asserters are bold, strong leaders who take charge and motivate others. They are objective, confident, and decisive, and they focus on delivering results at all costs. They are driven primarily by their need for power, and they strive to control their environment—including those they work and live with.

Often found in senior executive, finance, and military roles, asserters tend to be more formal and they appreciate recognition and compliance. They prefer a work environment where people, resources, and opportunities revolve around them, and they are more concerned with performance and results than with people and feelings. Despite the many action- and results-oriented positive benefits associated with asserters, when they sense a loss of control or a lack of appreciation from others their dark side can emerge (see Figure 5.2).

From an inclusion perspective, the common barriers, or what I refer to as *microtransgressions*, that leaders create and sustain, while subtle, can frustrate member engagement and candid communication. My research has focused on linking unique patterns of bias and microtransgressions to the unique leadership shadows.

Shadow bias, more commonly referred to as unconscious bias, refers to implicit or underlying biases that reside in our subconscious and very often impact our behavior without our conscious awareness. For the asserter style there are two primary patterns that need to be recognized: *confirmation bias* and the *over-confidence effect*. Figure 5.3 presents the asserter and fear of betrayal shadow bias cycle.

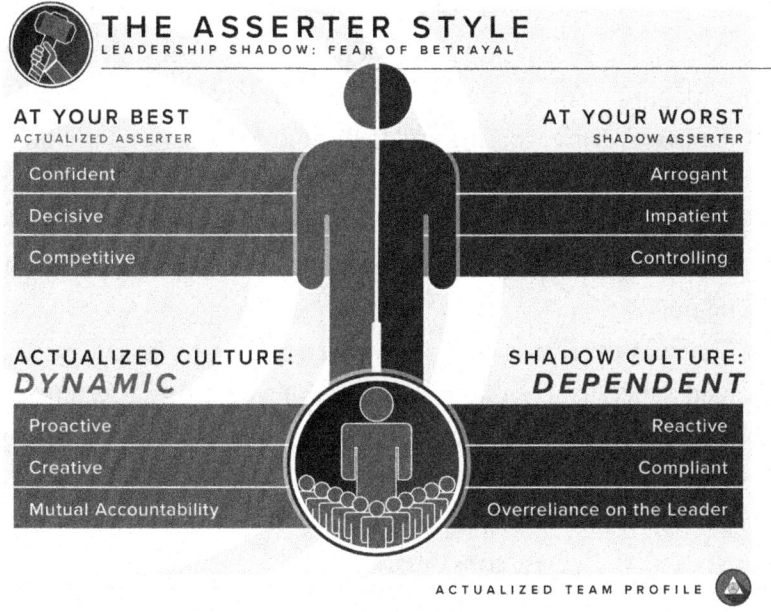

Figure 5.2. The asserter style

Figure 5.3. The asserter and fear of betrayal shadow bias cycle

Shadow Bias

Confirmation bias is the tendency to notice and acknowledge only data points that confirm your current point of view, opinion, or perspective—hence the name. For example, if you have a strong opinion about the capabilities or work ethic of an individual, positive or negative, you will tend to attend to and amplify only data that supports your opinion. For example, you may believe that Sue is a lazy individual because twice when you've tried to call her (after 5:00 p.m.) your calls have gone to voice mail. You may have overheard that she is a single parent and has a demanding schedule at home, but you discount or disregard that. Or, you may have a perspective that Roger is very hard-working and dedicated to your team and project. Chances are he is an asserter just like you and excels at managing up. At any rate, you are likely to excuse his tardiness or absence from team meetings thinking "something else more important must have come up."

The reason this is such an important bias to be aware of and manage is because it strikes at the heart of what many asserters relish: their ability to be objective and fair. This bias extends to more than just people. It also adversely impacts our ability to rationally appraise progress, situational factors, and other nuanced or even intuitive data points that merit consideration.

The *over-confidence effect* is exactly what it sounds like: the inherent tendency to have an overwhelming sense of confidence and pride in one's opinion, position, and ability. Asserters often overestimate their ability, which makes accepting constructive feedback extremely challenging. Moreover, this bias makes it even more difficult to be vulnerable, which is necessary for authenticity. Whether you need to ask for help or apologize, or be the first to say "I love you," this implicit bias leads to asserters building a wall that they think is for protection, until they realize (often too late) that their carefully laid bricks and mortar represent a prison preventing a basic human need we all have—authentic connection to others.

Microtransgressions

Common microtransgressions of the asserter style, which in this case are more commonly referred to as microaggressions, include interrupting others and employing a condescending tone to make their point. As Jerry Harvey taught me early on (see Chapter 1: "My F in Life" from *Actualized Leadership*), our need to win every battle often turns conversations and team discussions into mental chess matches. We strategize our approach, interrupting others when necessary to point out their flawed logic or violation of their own stated assumption in order to win the argument. But remember, you can win every argument and still lose the war.

An example of this was illustrated by a speaker at an event where I had just given the talk over lunch. Although he had not taken the ALP or read my book, he let the large group of insurance professionals know that he was an asserter. And, he said he wanted to recount a story about winning every battle but losing the war. He discussed his recent marriage and the balance between being a newlywed and the demands of the road on the public speaking and book promotion tour. The past weekend he had finally arrived home on a delayed flight, exhausted and, in his own words, "three or four drinks into the evening." Tired and cranky, he really was excited to see his wife, whom he had missed very much, and to spend the evening "doing what newlyweds do." However, his shadow was out in full force, and he immediately began critiquing his wife's decisions. *Why did you park so far away in the economy lot* (she apologized), *what were you thinking when you scheduled drinks on the way home with our neighbors* (she cancelled), and *why hadn't you had the cable service restored* (she also worked a demanding job)? This gentleman was right on every point, and his wife apologized each time. And he said, as he fell asleep on the couch that night because he had been uninvited out of the bedroom, the realization that he had lost the war came crashing down on him.

In addition to interrupting others, the use of a condescending tone is a subtle microtransgression that is used to demean others. Common examples include "do I need to explain this to you?" or "have you already forgotten what we talked about?" and serve the purpose of knocking the other party off-balance, allowing for greater ease in maneuvering the conversation to a successful win. But asserters should take heed, because this approach creates resentment and anger in others, and although they may be too scared to show it, it's there. And quite often, they will abandon ship, moving to another team or another organization, to get away from this tone. To the asserter, this feels like a betrayal, the core fear of their leadership shadow. But when assessed honestly (and objectively), they must take responsibility for their own hand in meeting their destiny.

Leadership Shadow: Fear of Betrayal

Unlike affirmers, who may put their need for connection and acceptance over everything else, asserters always want to be right and will ride roughshod over those who dare to challenge them. The stress this creates triggers their fear of betrayal leadership shadow, and, as a result, their confidence becomes arrogance, control devolves into manipulation, and decisiveness becomes autocracy. This need for power and control creates dysfunction at work and at home and creates a culture of anxiety and fear.

As with achievers and affirmers, asserters are subject to a leadership shadow cycle of irrational thoughts that create unfounded feelings, and those feelings lead to shadow behaviors that are self-defeating, as illustrated in Figure 5.4.

When asserters devolve from confident, in control, and decisive to arrogant, manipulative, and autocratic, they may find that those around them eventually decide to look for a less difficult situation. And asserters will realize that by not understanding how

Irrational Thoughts	Unfounded Feelings	Self-Defeating Behaviors
I have to always be in charge	Control	Constantly maneuvering for more control and power
People cannot be trusted	Skeptical	Rarely putting your guard down or expressing vulnerability
I am right	Arrogance	Being outspoken, autocratic, and sarcastic

⇩

Unconscious Desire for Control and Independence

⇩

Leadership Trap: Pro-Dependent

⇩

Basic Assumptions	Group Emotions	Team Behaviors
Our leader knows best We need to be protected Rules and procedures provide safety and consistency	Fear and anxiety	Overreliance on the leader Lack of critical judgment Assumptions are not challenged Pleas for assistance and guidance Compliance over creativity

⇩

Results: Vulnerability and Codependence

Figure 5.4. The leadership shadow cycle: Asserter

to manage their leadership shadow, their biggest fear—betrayal—is lurking around the corner. Oftentimes, direct reports who have been berated or embarrassed one too many times eject at their first opportunity, and while their rationale is clear to others, the asserter can focus only on the overwhelming betrayal they feel. That feeling, in turn, makes asserters experience excruciating vulnerability.

What's Next

In Chapter 6, we will explore groupthink, the common group decision-making dysfunction that is found most often in the detached and dependent team cultures. The chapter will provide a detailed examination of the initial conditions that lead to groupthink, as well as the common symptoms associated with it. The chapter will close with suggested strategies for helping leaders and teams both identify and manage groupthink.

PART III

PITFALLS IN TEAM DECISION MAKING

Chapter 6

Groupthink and Managing Team Conflict

What's in this chapter?

» Irving Janis and Groupthink Defined
» Groupthink and the Detached and Dependent Team Cultures
» Identifying the Conditions and Characteristics of Groupthink
» Preventing and Managing the Dynamics of Groupthink
» What's Next

In the collective mind the intellectual aptitudes of the individuals, and in consequence their individuality, are weakened. The heterogenous is swamped by the homogeneous, and the unconscious qualities obtain the upper hand.

—Gustave Le Bon

THE BIG IDEA

Groupthink is a common team decision-making pitfall that occurs with groups are unable to manage their conflict productively. Groupthink is most likely to occur when the culture is detached or dependent, and overt pressure is used to coerce members towards consensus. Strategies to prevent groupthink include addressing the team's leader's shadow, appointing members to play devil's advocate, and creating a less formal, more open climate where conflict can be more effectively managed.

CLASSIC EXAMPLES OF GROUPTHINK

Classic examples from history include the Bay of Pigs Invasion and the National Aeronautic and Space Administration's (NASA) decision to launch the Challenger in 1986.

Bay of Pigs Invasion

The chain of events leading up to the failed Bay of Pigs invasion of Cuba in 1961, where US-trained and equipped soldiers attempted to overthrow Fidel Castro, is a classic example of groupthink. President John F. Kennedy wanted to overthrow Castro, and his subordinates knew it because he inserted himself directly into the deliberation. As a result, his group was not thinking rationally or objectively. Instead, they jumped to conclusions, self-censored, and embraced recommendations that almost led to conflict with the former Soviet Union.

1986 NASA Challenger Tragedy

Prior to the launch of Challenger in 1986, Morton Thiokol engineers, who were responsible for manufacturing the O-rings for the booster rockets, expressed concern about the O-rings sealing quickly enough at the predicted lower temperatures. NASA administrators applied direct pressure on the engineers to recommend a launch, based on perceived media pressure due to recent delays. Although the engineers had serious concerns, they gave in to the pressure and recommended the launch, which led to a disastrous end.

As previously defined, teams are *three or more individuals who share a common goal and meet on a frequent basis to share information, solve problems, and capture emerging opportunities.* At the heart of team performance and productivity is decision-making—*group decision-making*, to be exact. The lifeblood for an effective group decision-making climate is communication: open, honest, and candid communication without fear of reprisal and retribution. Sounds easy enough, right? But as you well know, in practice it is very difficult. Social pressure (real or imagined), fear of separation, and self-censorship are just some of the factors that impede rational and effective group decision-making. Over the next two chapters we will explore the two classic pitfalls in group decision-making: groupthink and the Abilene paradox. While there are some similarities between the two, there are important differences that underly these dysfunctional decision-making phenomena. The inability to manage conflict, which occurs in the detached and dependent cultures, lies at the heart of groupthink. The inability to manage agreement, which occurs in the dramatic and dependent cultures, lies at the heart of the Abilene paradox. This chapter will focus on groupthink and will provide suggestions for both identifying and managing this team dysfunction and, in doing so, preventing groupthink from occurring in your team and organization.

Irving Janis and Groupthink Defined

Examples of groupthink abound in our society. From historical examples such as NASA's decision to launch Challenger, Pearl Harbor, the Bay of Pigs invasion, and Watergate, to more recent examples such as the 2008 housing collapse, the ice bucket challenge, and the cancel culture that thrives in our society today, we see numerous and diverse examples of groups and even nations making collective decisions that lack thoughtful challenge and rational appraisal.

From a business perspective, there are too many examples to cite. Whether we consider well-known examples such as the collapse of Enron or Kodak's refusal to enter the digital camera market, or countless decisions by boards to merge two organizations or an executive team supporting a sacred cow initiative doomed to failure, the tendency for groups to engage in groupthink seems to be ubiquitous.

In 1972, Yale University's Dr. Irving Janis identified groupthink as a mode of thinking that occurs when a group's strong desire for cohesion and unanimity prevents it from realistically appraising other alternatives or options. Oftentimes, conformity or peer pressure ensues so that any group member who voices dissent is quickly reminded that the group norm is consent. Janis defines groupthink as "a mode of thinking that people engage in when they are deeply involved in a cohesive in-group, when members' strivings for unanimity override their motivation to realistically appraise alternative courses of action." He adds, "groupthink refers to a deterioration of mental efficiency, reality testing, and moral judgment that results from in-group pressures" (1972).

Groupthink and the Detached and Dependent Team Cultures

Culture ultimately determines the degree of communication, the level of member engagement, and the quality of decision-making. Teams with less-than-optimal cultures generally fall into one of two extreme categories:

» *Detached*, cold and angry, or
» *Dramatic*, warm and friendly.

These two distinct and very different cultures result in two very different dynamics and processes, but they ultimately lead to the same outcome: a bad decision. Please note that the most common culture I've observed in my thirty years of applied research and consulting is dependent, which was previously discussed in Chapter 5. Essentially, I have found that a dependent culture is as likely to lead to groupthink as to trips to Abilene depending on the context and style of leader (asserter style can be either a benevolent dictator [the Abilene paradox] or more autocratic [groupthink]).

How a team arrives at the decision is a function of the underlying culture. Detached cultures facilitate conflict, passive and aggressive, and a team's inability to manage this conflict often results in the dysfunction of groupthink. Teams with a dramatic culture, warm and friendly but lacking in candor, are often unable to manage their agreement and suffer from the Abilene paradox. The travel routes of groupthink and the Abilene paradox are very different, but the destination—a poor decision—is the same (see Figure 6.1).

Dysfunctional group decision-making: Groupthink and the Abilene paradox

Teams that are detached or dependent are often unable to manage their conflict and, as a result, are victims of groupthink.

Decision-Making Dysfunction	Common Attributes	Outcome
Groupthink	Ineffective communication Actual pressure to conform	Inability to manage conflict
The Abilene paradox	Ineffective communication Perceived pressure to conform	Inability to manage agreement

Figure 6.1. Dysfunctional group decision-making: Detached or dependent teams

Teams that have devolved into an angry or apathetic detached culture exhibit groupthink behaviors such as resignment, open conflict, and ridicule. In general, groupthink occurs when groups are frustrated and ineffective in managing conflict and so focus on pressuring members to "get with the program" or "be a team player."

A dramatic culture is characterized by the exact opposite group dynamics. In this culture, conflict and candor are replaced by warm agreement and self-censorship. Unfortunately, both cultures guarantee poor decision-making since the false consensus exhibited by a dramatic culture leads the team to take inappropriate actions. This false consensus, characterized as the Abilene paradox, will be discussed in Chapter 7.

Identifying the Conditions and Characteristics of Groupthink

Before we examine the symptoms that often lead to teams engaging in groupthink, it is important to examine the initial conditions that often impact team decision making. While team culture is very real, it exists in the larger context of the organizational or corporate culture. And even beyond that, companies and organizations operate in the larger zeitgeist of the global business and political hyperconnected world we live in today. Some of the more common initial conditions that often impact group decision making are:

- » High team cohesiveness,
- » Insulation of the team from outsiders (both within and outside the organization),
- » Lack of formal and transparent procedures for appraisal of options and alternatives,
- » Highly directive leadership, achievers and asserters,
- » High stress with a low degree of hope for finding a better solution than the one favored by the leader or other individuals influencing the decision-making process, and
- » Complex and ambiguous environment.

In addition to these initial conditions, there are some easily observable behavior dimensions that suggest groupthink may be occurring. For example, once a position is outlined by someone with power or authority on the team, everyone focuses on why the position is the right one. No one raises objections. If different perspectives are offered, they are quickly dismissed, and options that were rejected during discussion are never revisited. Finally, information that might challenge the team's assumptions is not actively sought or considered.

Beyond these initial conditions, which seem quite common in my experience, eight symptoms of groupthink have been identified, and the more of these characteristics that exist, the more likely it is that your team will be a victim of groupthink.

The characteristics of groupthink include the following points:

- » An *illusion of invulnerability* is shared by most or all team members, which creates excessive optimism and encourages taking extreme risks. Statements such as "No one can stop us now" often are made by members suffering from an illusion of invulnerability.

» *Collective rationalization* discounts warnings that might lead the members to reconsider their assumptions before committing themselves to major policy decisions.

» An *unquestioned belief* in the team's inherent morality leads members to ignore the ethical or moral consequences of their decisions.

» *Stereotypical views* of rivals and enemies (other groups) picture them as too evil to warrant genuine attempts to negotiate or too weak or stupid to counter whatever attempts are made to defeat their purpose.

» *Direct pressure* is exerted on any member who expresses strong arguments against any of the team's illusions, stereotypes, or commitments, making clear that such dissent is contrary to what is expected of all loyal members. The leader might say, "Get with the program" or "There's no 'I' in team."

» *Self-censorship* of deviations from any apparent team consensus reflects the inclination of members to minimize the importance of their doubts and not present counterarguments. A member might think, "If everyone feels that way, my feelings must be wrong" or "They have more experience than I do and, as such, must know something that I don't."

» A *shared illusion of unanimity* results, in part, from self-censorship and is reinforced by the false assumption that silence implies consent.

» The emergence of self-appointed *mind-guard* members serves to protect the team from additional information or emerging data or trends that might shatter the shared complacency about the effectiveness and morality of their decisions.

In a recent study of twenty-three top management teams, the chief executive officers (CEOs) of more than 25 percent of these teams expressed concerns about groupthink. The CEOs of a large financial retailing company and a global financial services firm commented:

> *We're all too much on the same wavelength. We were all part of a management buyout four years ago. We've been through some tough battles together, and now we share a lot of common views. But in this industry, you have to be fresh and experimental. If we all agree on everything, how new or exciting can our ideas be?*
>
> *There's a lack of genuine debate. Sometimes there's a half-hearted devil's advocate gesture, but they really don't confront each other or me on the big issues. We're too comfortable, too self-congratulatory. It's gotten obvious to me in the past few months. I have to find a way to shake things up.*

Figure 6.2 illustrates the process of groupthink and the various factors impacting group decision making.

Preventing and Managing the Dynamics of Groupthink

Groupthink isn't inevitable, and several steps can be taken to either remedy it or avoid it altogether. Before examining some of these practical strategies for improving group decision making, let's explore three general attributes that have significant impact on both team culture and group decision making. These three factors contribute to the overall culture and group dynamics of the team, including the size, cohesiveness, and diversity of the team. Each will be discussed as it relates to group decision-making.

Very often I get asked "what size should my team be?" Obviously, the size of a team varies and is based on a number of factors. What is critical to remember is that a trade-off occurs from a group dynamics perspective when the size of the team increases. *Social loafing* is the

Initial Conditions
» High cohesiveness
» Insulation of the team from outsiders
» Lack of process and procedures for calibrating external factors
» Directive (achiever or asserter) leadership
» Stressful environment with a high sense of urgency for making a decision or recommendation
» Complex and rapidly changing environment

Conformity-Seeking Tendency of Group

Characteristics of Groupthink
» Illusion of invulnerability
» Collective rationalization
» Belief in inherent morality of the team
» Stereotypes of other groups
» Direct pressure on dissenters
» Self-censorship
» Illusion of unanimity
» Self-appointed *mind guards*

Groupthink Leads to Defective Decision-Making
» Incomplete review of alternatives
» Lack of goal clarity
» Failure to examine exposure and potential risks of favored solution
» Invalid or incomplete information
» Confirmation bias in processing information
» Failure to revisit other options
» Lack of contingency planning

Figure 6.2. The process of groupthink

concept used to describe a common and less-than-optimal aspect related to group decision making: *as the size of the team increases, individual member engagement and participation decreases.* This applies to all group settings, and it isn't personal; it just is. This finding, sometimes referred to as the *free rider tendency*, is a natural outcome of group behavior. As the size of the group increases, members believe that someone else will know more or do more to provide a solution, suggestion, or recommendation for a given issue. As previously stated, there are many and diverse reasons for increasing the size of your team. You need to carefully weigh those advantages, however, against the very real dangers posed by this phenomenon. As a general rule of thumb, I suggest determining the smallest number of members your team could be, and then subtracting one.

Team cohesiveness refers to how committed the members are to each other and to the organization they serve. Not surprisingly, as group cohesiveness increases, so too does productivity, performance, and, in a reinforcing cycle, member engagement. Teams that suffer from a lack of cohesiveness often have developed a detached or dependent culture, where members have different agendas, ambiguous goals, or are part of a group that is too large in number. Several factors, such as frequent interactions, getting together outside of the office (either socially or onsite with a plant or facility location), and a clear goal or challenge can increase a sense of cohesiveness and, in doing so, create a more dynamic culture. Sometimes a common enemy, such as a hostile takeover bid or competitor, will also facilitate a rapid sense of cohesion.

Diversity is the third factor that informs and impacts group decision making. Diversity in every sense—race, gender, skill set, experience, opinions, and perspectives—will help ensure that your team matches the complexity and diversity of our global market. A note of caution: diversity and heterogeneity often lower performance in the short term. When team members see things differently or don't feel they are on the same page there is a lag of performance. However, research demonstrates that over time these differences move from being tolerated to being appreciated, and they help teams make thoughtful, reasoned decisions in an increasingly complex and diverse global economy.

Let's explore some evidence-based strategies for preventing groupthink. First, we need to consider how cohesively our team operates. Research consistently demonstrates that teams with a moderate amount of cohesiveness produce better decisions than low- or high-cohesive teams. Teams with low cohesiveness are disengaged and typically operate in a detached culture. Alternatively, highly cohesive teams with strong ties to, and admiration for, the leader typically operate in a dependent culture. Perhaps not surprisingly, the high cohesiveness that dysfunctional dependency often produces actually leads to the poorest decisions, despite high confidence in those decisions demonstrated by both the leader (asserter) and the team.

Groupthink, identified and acknowledged, can be managed and even avoided if teams are willing to have an open, honest dialogue about the issue. Recognition and acknowledgement are key first steps, but alone they are not enough to prevent groupthink. Teams will often resist the diagnosis of culture and the corresponding emotionality associated with each. For example, a detached culture must come to grips with the fight/flight response that is being manifested at a group level. This response is grounded in the emotions of anger and apathy, where the team acts out on tacit (as-if) assumptions that there is an enemy out there that must be defeated. I've had my interpretations of a detached culture met with clients slamming their fists on the table while insisting "I'm not angry!" The micromanaging style, what *Harvard Business Review* authors Luis Velasquez and Kristin Gleitsman refer to as "umbrella managers," creates detachment instead of engagement, resentment instead of admiration, and failure instead of success.

Likewise, the dependent culture interpretation involves the team and the leader acknowledging a dysfunctional pattern grounded in fear and anxiety. The team must acknowledge that they are over-relying on the leader for direction and guidance while being afraid to challenge their assumptions or disagree with the group norm. And, just as importantly, if not more so, the leader (asserter) must acknowledge and own that they receive intrinsic satisfaction from being in charge and having the last word in every aspect of the group's operations. As the late, great Dr. Jerry Harvey used to say, you can't have a dependent team without a pro-dependent leader. The fear for the asserter style is betrayal and the remedy is to be in total control. The tragic and paradoxical irony, however, is that they will almost certainly lose control, and resent being overly relied upon by the team.

But take heart! It's not all doom and gloom. Groups can radically transform their cultures in a matter of moments when both the leader and the team have the courage to acknowledge and break their dysfunctional patterns. Once this has occurred, there are a number of practical strategies for alleviating or preventing groupthink:

1. The leader should avoid stating preferences and expectations at the outset. Rather, they should listen first (ask questions) and avoid putting their position in the room too soon.
2. Each member of the group should be assigned the role of critical evaluator. This role involves actively voicing objectives and doubts, even if (or perhaps especially if) it relates to an alternative or course of action suggested by the member taking on the role. I have found this approach to be especially useful as it is not personal and is shared among all team members.
3. Engage external experts (e.g., chief financial officers [CFOs], industry experts, etc.) to provide critical reactions to potential solutions, as well as additional environmental and macro context for the team that might have a material impact on deliberations and discussions.
4. Different groups with different leaders should explore the same issues and questions and work independently from each other in order to reach novel solutions and proposed courses of action.

5. Once a consensus has been reached, everyone should be encouraged to rethink their position to check for flaws. As my late mentor Dr. Dominic J. Monetta used to say, employ the "donut concept" and focus on the hole—"what's missing, or what has been assumed and not challenged?"

What's Next

Chapter 7 provides a detailed description and discussion of the group decision-making dysfunction known as the Abilene paradox, which represents a team's inability to manage agreement. The chapter begins with an overview of the paradox and describes the various symptoms that lead to mismanaged agreement, primarily in the dramatic and dependent team cultures. The chapter offers remedies and strategies for managing this dysfunction.

Chapter 7

The Abilene Paradox and Managing Team Agreement

What's in this chapter?

» Jerry Harvey and the Abilene Paradox Defined
» Trips to Abilene and the Dramatic and Dependent Team Cultures
» Identifying the Conditions and Characteristics of the Abilene Paradox
» Preventing and Managing the Dynamics of the Abilene Paradox
» What's Next

The work and emotional components of group life are so interrelated that one never occurs without the other.

—Herbert A. Thelen

THE BIG IDEA

The Abilene paradox, also known as "trips to Abilene," is a very common team decision-making pitfall that occurs with groups are unable to manage their agreement. A trip to Abilene is most likely to occur when the culture is dramatic or dependent, where negative fantasies and action anxiety prevent team members from voicing their true beliefs and feelings. Strategies for preventing the Abilene paradox include addressing the team's leader's shadow, encouraging members to communicate honestly and directly with each other and to address any white elephants (i.e., obvious problems) impacting the team's decision-making processes and performance.

In the previous chapter, we reviewed the classic concept of group-think, first identified by Dr. Irving Janis in the early 1970s, that is based on peer or conformity pressure applied to group members. Jerry B. Harvey challenged the notion that poor decision-making is always the result of groupthink in his seminal 1974 article "The Abilene Paradox: Mismanaged Agreement." According to Harvey's research, groups don't always make poor decisions because of peer pressure. Instead, Harvey wrote, groups often make poor decisions due to a failure of individual members to communicate honestly and directly with each other. It is important to note that Jerry Harvey's doctoral dissertation research (Ph.D. in social psychology from the University of Texas, Austin) actually focused on peer pressure and resulting poor decisions and adverse actions that follow. In other words, his dissertation research supported the groupthink frame-work for dysfunctional group decision-making. In personal commu-nication to me, he stated that he "tossed his dissertation on the altar of peer pressure" to try and explain (and to a certain degree, excuse) group behavior. Later, he disavowed his research for two reasons. First, he believed that it absolved individuals from taking personal responsibility for their decisions and their actions. In essence, at the heart of conformity or peer pressure is "the group made me do it." Citing Erich Fromm's *Escape from Freedom* and the need for psycho-logical health and maturity, he believed that we must take responsi-bility for our actions. It's important to note that he also spent a great deal of time and energy discussing (and writing about) forgiveness and the human need to both seek and award forgiveness.

The second reason he disavowed his dissertation is because the more he conducted research into group decision-making, the less he found occurrences of actual overt peer or conformity pressure. Rather, he uncovered personal separation anxiety and self-censorship, as opposed to interpersonal threats or pressure, that led to poor group decisions. In other words, he believed that the majority of poor group decisions were the result of mismanaged agreement—not conflict.

For sure I think there are numerous examples to support both groupthink (actual pressure and mismanaged conflict) as well as trips to Abilene (separation anxiety and mismanaged agreement) as valid frameworks for understanding why reasonably normal and intelligent people often act like nincompoops in group settings. This chapter will focus on the latter and will examine why we get on the road to Abilene as well as explore ways to skip the trip.

Jerry Harvey and the Abilene Paradox Defined

Having worked closely with Jerry for years as a doctoral student and having stayed in touch with him until his passing in 2015 (and still in contact with his wife Beth Harvey), I came to realize that Jerry was a truly gifted storyteller. His unique ability to spin a yarn with both dry humor and profound insight always made me think of the Dr. Seuss-like quality of his meditations on management. My experience reading his work, or talking to him directly, was to be laughing one moment, and then shaking my head ruminating on a profound insight about human behavior that often hit a little too close to home. In other words, Harvey's words, whether written or spoken, connected with me (and I would confidently say many, many others) on a deeply personal level that wasn't always comfortable. And that was exactly his point. Human growth—personal transformation—can come only from experiencing the trepidation and anxiety created by confronting our shadow. Harvey wasn't in the incremental or continuous improvement business. He was in the personal, group, and organization transformation line of work. But he never lost sight of the fact that irrespective of the unit of analysis (individual, group, or organization) all three comprised people just like you and me. And to Harvey's way of thinking, storytelling was the most effective way to engage an audience and, ultimately, to create the conditions or invitation for transformation. So, to that end, I will present the Abilene paradox in Harvey's own words. The following is taken directly from his classic organizational dynamics article in 1974, "The Abilene Paradox: Mismanaged Agreement."

> July Sunday afternoons in Coleman, Texas (population 5,607), are not exactly winter holidays. This one was particularly hot—104 degrees as measured by the Walgreens Rexall Ex-Lax Temperature Gauge located under the tin awning that covered a rather substantial screened-in back porch. In addition, the wind was blowing fine-grained West Texas topsoil through the house. The windows were closed, but dust filtered through what were apparently cavernous but invisible openings in the walls.
>
> "How could dust blow through closed windows and solid walls?" one might ask. Such a question betrays more of the provincialism of the reader than the writer. Anyone who has ever lived in West Texas wouldn't bother to ask. Just let it be said that wind can do a lot of things with topsoil when more than thirty days have passed without rain.
>
> But the afternoon was still tolerable—even potentially enjoyable. A water-cooled fan provided adequate relief from the heat as long as one didn't stray too far from it, and we didn't. In addition, there was cold lemonade for sipping. One might have preferred stronger stuff, but Coleman was "dry" in more ways than one; and so were my in-laws, at least until someone got sick. Then a teaspoon or two for medicinal purposes might be legitimately considered. But this particular Sunday no one was ill; and anyway, lemonade seemed to offer the necessary cooling properties we sought.
>
> And finally, there was entertainment. Dominoes. Perfect for the conditions. The game required little more physical exertion than an occasional mumbled comment, "shuffle 'em," and an unhurried movement of the arm to place the spots in the appropriate perspective on the

table. It also required somebody to mark the score; but that responsibility was shifted at the conclusion of each hand so the task, though onerous, was in no way physically debilitating. In short, dominoes was diversion, but pleasant diversion.

So, all in all it was an agreeable—even exciting— Sunday afternoon in Coleman; if, to quote a contemporary radio commercial, "You are easily excited." That is, it was until my father-in-law suddenly looked up from the table and said with apparent enthusiasm, "Let's get in the car and go to Abilene and have dinner at the cafeteria."

To put it mildly, his suggestion caught me unprepared. You might even say it woke me up. I began to turn it over in my mind. "Go to Abilene? Fifty-three miles? In this dust storm? We'll have to drive with the lights on even though it's the middle of the afternoon. And the heat. It's bad enough here in front of the fan but in an unairconditioned 1958 Buick it will be brutal. And eat at the cafeteria? Some cafeterias may be okay, but the one in Abilene conjures up dark memories of the enlisted men's field mess."

But before I could clarify and organize my thoughts even to articulate them, Beth, my wife, chimed in with, "Sounds like a great idea. I would like to go. How about you, Jerry?" Well, since my own preferences were obviously out of step with the rest, I decided not to impede the party's progress and replied with, "Sounds good to me," and added, "I just hope your mother wants to go."

"Of course I want to go," my mother-in-law replied. "I haven't been to Abilene in a long time. What makes you think I wouldn't want to go?"

So into the car and to Abilene we went. My predictions were fulfilled. The heat was brutal. We were coated with a fine layer of West Texas dust, which was cemented with perspiration by the time we arrived; and the food at the cafeteria provided first-rate testimonial material for Alka-Seltzer commercials.

Some four hours and 106 miles later we returned to Coleman, Texas, but tired and exhausted. We sat in front of the fan for a long time in silence. Then, both to be sociable and also to break a rather oppressive silence, I said, "It was a great trip, wasn't it?"

No one spoke.

Finally, my mother-in-law said, with some slight note of irritation, "Well, to tell the truth, I really didn't enjoy it much and would have rather stayed here. I just went along because the three of you were so enthusiastic about going. I wouldn't have gone if you all hadn't pressured me into it."

I couldn't believe it. "What do you mean 'you all'?" I said. "Don't put me in the 'you all' group. I was delighted to be doing what we were doing. I didn't want to go. I only went to satisfy the rest of you characters. You are the culprits."

Beth looked shocked. "Don't call me a culprit. You and Daddy and Mama were the ones who wanted to go. I just went along to be sociable and to keep you happy. I would have had to be crazy to want to go out in heat like that. You don't think I'm crazy, do you?"

Before I had the opportunity to fall into that obvious trap, her father entered the conversation again with some abruptness. He spoke only one word, but he did it in the quite simple, straightforward vernacular that only a lifelong Texan and particularly a Colemanite can approximate. That word was "H-E-L-L."

Since he seldom resorted to profanity, he immediately caught our attention. Then he proceeded to expand on what was already an absolutely clear thought with,

"Listen, I never wanted to go to Abilene. I was sort of making conversation. I just thought you might have been bored, and I felt I ought to say something. I didn't want you and Jerry to have a bad time when you visit. You visit so seldom I wanted to be sure you enjoy it. And I knew Mama would be upset if you all didn't have a good time. Personally, I would have preferred to play another game of dominoes and eaten the leftovers in the icebox."

After the initial outburst of recrimination, we all sat back in silence. Here we were, four reasonably sensible people who, on our own volitions, had just taken a 106-mile trip across a Godforsaken desert in furnace-like temperatures through a cloudlike dust storm to eat unpalatable food at a hole-in-the-wall cafeteria in Abilene, Texas, when none of us really wanted to go. In fact, to be more accurate, we'd done just the opposite of what we wanted to do. The whole situation seemed paradoxical. It simply didn't make sense.

Trips to Abilene and the Dramatic and Dependent Team Cultures

As discussed in the previous chapter, the underlying culture of a team determines the processes that impact group decision making. Dramatic cultures facilitate warm and friendly relationships where their personal dynamic often trumps the performance outcome. Communication in this culture is often supportive and surface-level, so that underlying issues, obvious problems, or white elephants are ignored. The lack of candor and authenticity in this dynamic breeds frustration and even despair, and the team's inability to manage this agreement often results in the dysfunction of the Abilene paradox. As previously stated, while the team dynamics and underlying cultures that facilitate either groupthink or the Abilene paradox are very different, the destination—a poor decision—is the same.

A dramatic culture is characterized by warm agreement, positive personal relationships, and a certain degree of either sugar-coating the truth or outright self-censorship. This dynamic is tied to the affirmer style, where the fear of rejection leadership shadow emerges at the team level. As such, there is a heightened sense of wanting to stay connected to others and, therefore, a heightened degree of fear of separation. It's important to note that at a primal or existential level, we all have some degree of separation anxiety because some degree of connection to others is necessary for happiness and fulfillment, if not outright survival. In the dramatic culture, however, this team shadow has usurped the rational and conscious element of group work (dynamic culture) and has the upper hand. The resulting and observable behavioral manifestations of the dramatic culture are polite conversation, supportive comments, and group-level agreement to go to Abilene while privately individuals do not want to go.

As stated in the previous chapter, the dependent culture is the most common culture I've observed in my thirty years of applied research and consulting. The follow-the-leader dynamics of the dependent culture were previously discussed in Chapter 5. Essentially, I have found that a dependent culture is as likely to lead to groupthink as trips to Abilene, depending on the context and style of leader. The asserter style can control others by be either being a benevolent dictator, which leads to trips to Abilene, or by taking a more autocratic approach that creates unresolved conflict and the dynamics of groupthink (see Figure 7.1).

Identifying the Conditions and Characteristics of the Abilene Paradox

Just like with the decision-making dynamics of groupthink, the Abilene paradox has a number of conditions and characteristics that

Dysfunctional group decision-making: Groupthink and the Abilene paradox		
Teams that are detached or dependent are often unable to manage their conflict and, as a result, are victims of groupthink.		
Decision-Making Dysfunction	**Common Attributes**	**Outcome**
Groupthink	Ineffective communication Actual pressure to conform	Inability to manage conflict
The Abilene paradox	Ineffective communication Perceived pressure to conform	Inability to manage agreement

Figure 7.1. Dysfunctional group decision-making: Detached or dependent teams

lead to mismanaged agreement and poor decision-making. Following are the five most common conditions that facilitate trips to Abilene:

1. Members agree in a private (not a public) forum about the nature of the situation, and what they want to do.
2. Members fail to accurately communicate their thoughts, feelings, desires, and beliefs to each other in a team setting. This requires members to self-censor their true beliefs and feelings in order to "go with the flow" or "get on board" with the program.
3. Invalid and inaccurate information leads team members to make collective decisions that are contrary to their individual opinions and views.
4. The team agrees on a decision or course of action based on faulty information that no one privately supports.
5. Team members experience frustration, anger, irritation, and dissatisfaction over poor decisions that range from less-than-optimal to disastrous.

Jerry Harvey remarked that it is "pretty absurd isn't it, people taking actions in contradiction to what they really want to do?" Yet, most of us can cite more than a few examples of this group decision-making process occurring. Harvey eventually identified the psychological and group dynamic principles that enable the Abilene paradox to draw its enormous power, as listed here:

» **Action anxiety**: One of drama's most famous characters, Hamlet, famously mused, "To be or not to be, that is the question" as he pondered suicide. Action anxiety occurs when we are unsure of which action to take; we often shut down and do nothing.

» **Negative fantasies**: Negative fantasies are the dire, predicted outcomes we mentally construct which provide a basis and justification for not speaking up or dissenting with the group. Such fantasies often range from thinking you might be ostracized from the team to fearing you may be demoted, removed from the team, or even fired.

» **Fear of separation**: A primal, existential fear of being alone or being separated from others often motivates us to agree to a course of action in a group setting when we privately have concerns or misgivings. As Harvey correctly illustrates, giving in to this fear often leads to experiencing what Viktor Frankl referred to as paradoxical intent and what he called a paradox within a paradox: the more you fear something, the more likely you will experience it, including separation. As such, not speaking up and owning up to your true beliefs and feelings will eventually lead you to the separation you are trying so hard to avoid.

» **Real risk**: Real risk is at play when you depart from the group norm of agreement. Harvey referred to this risk as the price of admission for being human and acknowledged that sometimes the fear of being ostracized, of not being a team player, or even losing your job, must be weighed accurately and objectively in deciding to voice your true opinions.

If you are currently in a group setting that is on the road to Abilene, some of the more subjective experiences identified below may resonate with you as you attempt to cope with the problem of mismanaged agreement. The more of these conditions listed here that you have or are currently experiencing, then the more likely you are in the middle of the Abilene paradox.

» You feel pained, frustrated, and basically helpless and unable to cope when trying to solve a particular organizational problem or meet a current challenge.

» You frequently meet with trusted colleagues and coworkers over coffee, clandestine lunches, or at the local pub to commiserate and to plan courses of action to try and remedy the situation.

» You blame others, and especially your boss who seems to support the solution, for the dilemma. The boss, in particular, frequently gets an unequal share of the blame and is responsible for this mess in the first place.

» In the actual team meetings when the problem is discussed you are more cautious, less than candid, vague, neutral, or even mildly supportive when discussing the issue or problem and its solution. As such, you are trying to determine what others' positions on the issues are without clearly revealing your own.

As these scenarios play out, your level of frustration dramatically increases, while your level of trust in others (both your manager and your teammates) dramatically decreases. It's only when the team or organization arrives in Abilene that you, totally exasperated, will exclaim "I never wanted to go in the first place!" And when the chief executive officer (CEO) wants to know who is responsible, you can rest assured you have arrived at your destination.

Preventing and Managing the Dynamics of the Abilene Paradox

Up to this point we've described the dynamics of mismanaged agreement in group decision-making and the psychological forces that make this experience all too common. But take heart, Harvey offers remedies for helping us to both diagnose when we may be getting on the road to Abilene, as well as strategies we can employ to help prevent (skip the trip) the process from playing out.

Diagnosing the Abilene Paradox

As with groupthink, there are recognizable symptoms of the Abilene paradox that, once identified, can be managed. Harvey recommends the following norms and ground rules to help groups avoid the Abilene paradox:

» Establish and reinforce the norm of collegial candor, not politeness.
» Treat conflict as not only normal, but necessary, to make optimal decisions and achieve synergy in a group setting.
» Establish the ground rule that everyone must participate and total engagement in the process is not only expected but required.
» Avoid being insulated. Bring in outsiders from time to time to provide expert input and analysis.
» Don't rush a major decision. Time is a reflection of priorities; when a major decision, such as strategic direction or succession planning, is in order, take the necessary time to reach a reasoned and thoughtful decision.

Preventing Future Trips to Abilene

Once the immediate problem of specific hidden agreements has been faced, the next step for the team is to voice their true beliefs and feelings so that the dysfunction can be broken. Next, the team should take care to establish a more formal and transparent process that will reduce the probability that similar problems will occur in the future. For example, I've worked with a number of teams that have simply employed that "Are we going to Abilene?" clause that anyone at any time can raise in a team meeting.

Underlying the paradox of collective consent to the trip to Abilene is fear of separation. Fear, in turn, is expressed through negative fantasies. For example, believing that you might get fired for speaking up is a common negative fantasy. Or it may be expressed as fear of a nonspecific group, such as top leadership, the CEO, or the board. Such fears can both contribute to and reinforce a general dysfunctional company culture maintained by myths, rumors, and exaggerations.

The following are a number of possible procedures that may help to either surface or prevent trips to Abilene:

» Appoint a devil's advocate to challenge proposed solutions and consensus.

» Engage an external consultant to interview people about unspoken concerns or to facilitate collegial candor sessions where concerns can be voiced. I have found that this process is especially impactful after either watching "The Abilene Paradox" video or sharing the article for pre-reading before the team meeting.

» Hold regular team-building sessions that focus on the process— the *how* and the *why* (as opposed to the task—the *what* and *by when*—that dominates most team meetings)—so that you can collectively exhale and check in to make sure that all voices are heard and concerns are identified sooner rather than later.

While these recommended steps can and do have a positive impact, the most fundamental issue that has to be addressed is a personal one: What am I afraid of and how important is it for me to be authentic and honest? In short, if the question of hidden agreement is to be truly solved, the question to be addressed is this: What skills can team members learn individually and collectively that will allow them to rise above any fear of separation and communicate honestly and authentically, with candor and sincerity? Your team's decision-making effectiveness, and ultimately your overall performance, depend on your answer.

What's Next

Chapter 8 begins Part 4 of the book, which is focused on team-actualization and optimizing performance. Chapter 8 explores the elements of a dynamic culture and what leaders and individual team members can do to help improve the sense of engagement and satisfaction among team members while enhancing team performance.

PART IV

Team-Actualization

Chapter 8

The Dynamic Culture

What's in this chapter?

» The Dynamic Culture in Action
» The Dynamic Culture Code: Greater or Equal to 75 Percent
» Characteristics of Dynamic Cultures and High-Performing Teams
» The Dynamic Culture: Actualized Leadership Style
» Team Dynamics and Leader Styles
» What's Next

You cannot merely expect culture to be a natural occurrence; it has to be taught and made part of your everyday routine.

—Mike "Coach K" Krzyzewski

THE BIG IDEA

The dynamic culture represents the highest level of team development and creates optimal member engagement and performance. It is within the dynamic culture that team-actualization—the process of the team reaching its collective potential—occurs. Dynamic cultures can be developed through team member awareness, developmental experiences, and an intentional, balanced focus on both people/relationships and performance/results. The desired score on the Dynamic scale on the actualized team profile (ATP) is greater than or equal to 75 percent.

Up to this point we have focused on shadows of teamwork and the dysfunctional group decision-making processes and suboptimal performance that they often create. As discussed in Chapter 2, there is always some degree of the rational, conscious aspect of group behavior (what I refer to as the dynamic culture) that works in concert with the shadow side of team culture. In fact, it is the dynamic and fluid interplay between the two—conscious and unconscious—that helps create and sustain the team culture. In this chapter we will turn our attention to the team-actualization process found in the dynamic culture where the group works at its highest collective potential and experiences synergistic performance outcomes as a result.

The Dynamic Culture in Action

Carmen is the General Counsel for an international manufacturing organization and oversees a myriad of complex and complicated legal challenges related to working in a global context. Based on the ALP Framework, she is an *actualized asserter*. When I first met her, I remember thinking "that's not what I expected." She has an Ivy League undergraduate degree and a law degree from a Top 10 program. She is very smart and very quick. In fact, I got the impression that she was two steps ahead of whomever she was talking to, including me. But I expected all of that. What I didn't expect was her informal, humble approach to working with others. Instead of talking about her accomplishments in college, she talked about working two part-time jobs to make ends meet. Instead of sitting at the head of the table when we met, she sat off to the side and invited me to sit at the head of the table. I noticed she had the same approach with her team. She was also very quick to admit mistakes and to laugh at them. She encouraged others to admit and own mistakes quickly so they could resolve them and move on.

After Carmen and her team had time to review their profile results and open-ended comments, she sincerely thanked everyone for their time. She acknowledged that she was proud, though not surprised, at the results. But then, she said it was time for the team to roll up their sleeves and get to work on how to improve. There was no self-congratulatory moment, no high-fives, just a sincere desire to improve. And she only had to ask once. Immediately team members began offering suggestions for improvement. They struck me as fairly minor, but I realized that Carmen and her team had, for the most part, gotten the really important stuff right. People felt comfortable speaking out without fear of retribution, even when they were disagreeing with Carmen. They were also so engaged in the process, and with the team, that what I thought might be a program that finished up a little early actually ran 45 minutes past our official end time. The other thing that really struck me was the sort of grounded, realistic optimism the team displayed. It was very obvious to me that they had had more than their fair share of battles in the trenches, and bonding from that was evident. There was genuine respect and collegiality in this team. They had a strong sense of purpose, as they made several comments about how their execution created jobs for real people with real families all over the world. Carmen had helped everyone look beyond a paycheck or a promotion; they were making a real difference in the communities they served, both at home and abroad. My final takeaway was the genuine comradery and festive spirit that spilled over into the resort bar after our meeting. The level of energy, engagement, and enthusiasm never waned, and as I tapped out early to catch my flight home, I remember thinking how refreshing it was to see the right balance between *performance and results* versus *people and relationships* that Carmen intentionally maintained, and how that flowed through to the team's balance on the task ("*What* are we working on?") and the process ("*How* are we working together?") (see Figure 2.4). Carmen and her team focused on both, not one at the expense of the other as so many teams often do. Their intentional efforts had created a dynamic culture where both positive results and positive engagement flowed.

Characteristics of Dynamic Cultures
and High-Performing Teams

There are numerous characteristics or attributes of high performing teams and the dynamic cultures that underlie their performance.
These qualities are listed here, and the Appendixes provide a number
of specific resources and strategies to help you and your team
develop, enhance, and improve these aspects of group life. While we
will also look at specific characteristics of dynamic performance by
leader style (i.e., achiever, affirmer and asserter) the following provide a good checklist for assessing your current team:

» Open, direct, and candid communication,
» Effective problem solving,
» Creativity,
» Resiliency,
» Grounded optimism,
» Shared leadership,
» Accountability,
» A learning lab setting for individual members,
» High engagement,
» Trust and mutual respect,
» Complex problems are broken down into more manage-
   able parts,
» Focused attention and staying on schedule,
» Conflict is managed constructively, often leading to better alter-
   natives and outcomes, and
» Sense of humor and comradery.

Chapter 9 will explore the five most crucial elements of culture—the 5 *dimensions of teamwork*—in detail. However, underlying
all five dimensions, and to some degree all of the above characteristics, is an assumption that team members know, understand, and
empathize with each other. In her book *The Right Call*, author Sally

Jenkins profiles a number of professional sports teams and coaches to better understand what produces winning teams and champions. She cites former San Francisco 49ers head coach Bill Walsh who spent time every training focused on players really getting to know each other. He wanted to ensure that any potential barriers, such as race, economic background, religion, and the like were knocked down before the season started so that the players really got to know and understand each other. Former 49ers quarterback Steve Young commented that Walsh wanted his players to know each other "an inch or two below the skin."

We see a similar approach in college athletics as well. The University of Georgia's (of which my wife Erin is a very proud alumnus) football team has had a very impressive run of late, winning (at the time of this writing) two out of the last three national championships in a row. Georgia's head coach Kirby Smart uses "skull sessions"—weekly gatherings that allow players to share their personal stories, fears, and motivations with each other—to help encourage players to let their guard down and be vulnerable with each other. These sessions were not added on as something *else* the team members had to do. The skull sessions were a part of their regular practice schedule and were convened instead of, or at the expense of, weightlifting or other normal practice activities.

As famed research and author Brené Brown reminds us in her now classic (and current record-holder for most viewed) TED Talk "The Power of Vulnerability," we can have authentic connection to others only if we have the courage to be vulnerable. Vulnerability is the critical component of empathy and deeper connection to others and can be cultivated in an environment where everyone feels seen and heard.

Senior offensive lineman Jamaree Salyer said his personal favorite topic of the skull sessions was "What's your why?" This topic allowed everyone to both explore and express their underlying drive and motivation for wanting to compete and excel at this elite level. In addition to really getting to know each other on a deeper level, he said it allowed the team to understand what made others tick and how to best motivate them on the field.

As previously discussed, the difference between task and process in team performance is often attended at the expense of the other. We spend most, if not all, of our time on the task—the *what* and *by when*. What is our goal, and when is it due? The other side of the coin, the process, focuses on the *how* and the *why*. How are we working together as a team, and why are we doing this? While most college football teams focus exclusively on the task, such as weight-lifting or scrimmaging, the skull sessions were designed and facilitated to focus on the process, the *how* and the *why*. In other words, the skull sessions were designed to build culture and community among the team. And just like Carmen's example at the beginning of this chapter, Coach Smart and the Georgia Bulldogs, and Bill Walsh and the San Francisco 49ers, demonstrate that by intentionally focusing our energy on both task and processes, we can create and sustain optimal performance and long-term success.

The Dynamic Culture: Actualized Leadership Style

Leaders, whether achievers, affirmers, or asserters, that are primarily driven by the need for self-actualization often exhibit seemingly contradictory approaches in their style of working with others. These apparently differing elements, however, are a result of attending to both relationship and results: people and performance. For example, they may be charismatic in a public setting but often long for solitude. Actualized leaders care deeply for their teammates and their organizations, but that does not inhibit them from making difficult decisions or providing real-time feedback. Unlike the affirmers who default to politeness, *actualized affirmers* default to candor. Unlike achievers who prefer routine and predictability, actualized achievers are spontaneous and enjoy novelty. And unlike asserters who crave control and trust others very slowly, actualized asserters humbly share their power and ask for input while implicitly trusting others to make decisions and take appropriate actions. While actualized leaders have a high need for achievement, care about their teammates, and are candid and decisive, they exhibit unique characteristics that create and sustain a dynamic team culture. For example, they understand the business but are not at all interested in getting bogged down in irrelevant details or trying to micromanage the board. They are strategic and conceptual, and they accept ambiguity and uncertainty as part of life. Actualized leaders tend to be more realistic and quicker to confront the brutal facts while trusting others and always being willing to ask for help, input, and guidance. While they often share many of the same characteristics of asserters, they use their power for the best interest of the organization as opposed to personal ego gratification. For example, they focus on the strategic objectives critical for success, but they do not feel compelled to be in control or to always be right. Finally, and perhaps most importantly, actualized leaders see the world from a sense of abundance as opposed to scarcity, and their motivation has a profound impact on creating a dynamic culture.

The aforementioned leadership qualities and approaches help create the highest performing team culture: dynamic. This culture is characterized by open, candid communication. Members have very high levels of engagement and are committed to both the organization and their teammates. Diverse opinions are not only tolerated, they are welcomed. Members are adept at questioning their own assumptions about the internal organization and the broader, external environment. They provide real-time, candid feedback to the leader and to each other in a respectful, collegial manner. Meetings are more efficient, because candor allows for honest discussions and debate, and more effective, because the team is able to focus on its primary objective and task.

While the more of these characteristics or attributes exist for a team, the greater the likelihood of a dynamic culture, there are unique qualities that typically abound with each of the three leader styles and corresponding shadow cultures: achiever/detached, affirmer/ dramatic, and asserter/dependent. The following section describes these unique aspects of teamwork by culture.

Team Dynamics and Leader Styles

Figure 8.1 illustrates the unique characteristics of a dynamic culture with an actualized achiever leader. While the *achieving dynamic team culture* will have many of the other characteristics previously outlined in this chapter, it will also have some specific qualities attributed to the achiever style, which include the following characteristics:

» Meetings tend to start and end on time, if not early.
» Members are intensely focused on the task at hand.
» The team has an overall mission or objective that aligns and energizes individual behavior.

Figure 8.1. The achiever style: Actualized

» Technical expertise and experience are shared openly and valued strongly.

» Members are fully engaged and the team often experiences flow.

» There is one agenda or objective, and every member is rowing in the same direction.

Figure 8.2 illustrates the unique characteristics of a dynamic culture with an actualized affirmer leader. While the *affirming dynamic team culture* will have many of the other characteristics previously outlined in this chapter, it will also have some specific qualities attributed to the affirmer style, which include the following characteristics:

» The team is supportive and constructive.

» Genuine empathy is shown for members' concerns and reservations.

» Communication is both relaxed and candid.

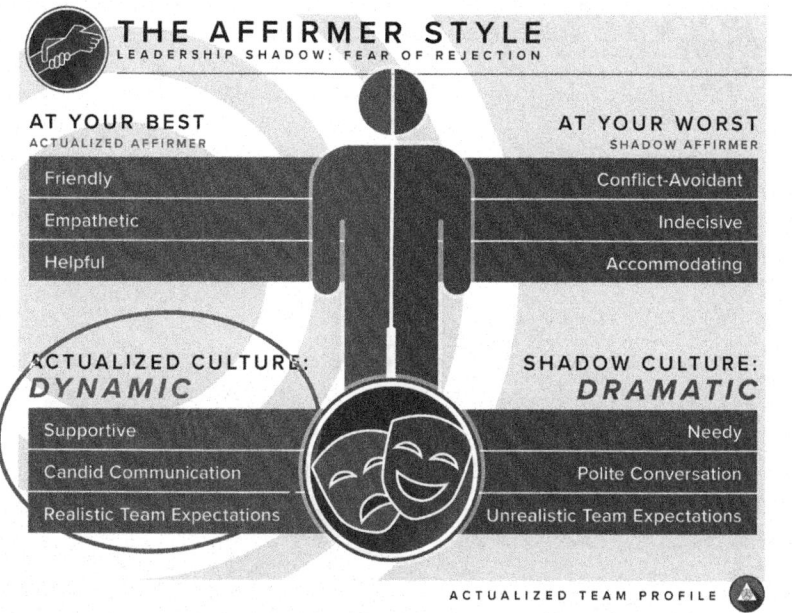

Figure 8.2. The affirmer style: Actualized

» Active listening abounds.

» The team is realistic and grounded in optimism for the future.

Figure 8.3 illustrates the unique characteristics of a dynamic culture with an actualized asserter leader. While the *asserting dynamic team culture* will have many of the other characteristics previously outlined in this chapter, it will also have some specific qualities attributed to the asserter style, which include the following characteristics:

» Members are proactive in their approach to problem solving.

» There is an informal and relaxed atmosphere.

» Creative and thoughtful suggestions and solutions are proposed.

» Members are comfortable giving constructive feedback and disagreeing with the leader.

» Mutual and shared accountability abounds among all team members.

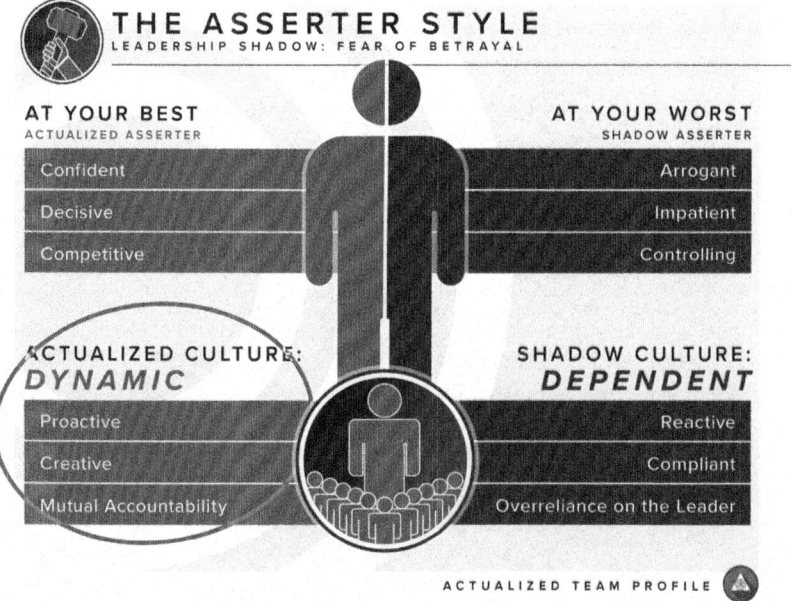

Figure 8.3. The asserter style: Actualized

What's Next

Chapter 9 outlines the five most important elements of working together in a team—the five dimensions of team performance. Each of these elements, communication, conflict management, engagement, purpose, and trust, is defined and illustrated with an interview from a respected business leader. Developmental resources for improving and enhancing each dimension are provided in both the chapter and the Appendixes.

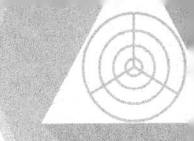

Chapter 9

The 5 Dimensions
of Teamwork

What's in this chapter?

> *So that's what destiny is: simply the fulfillment of the*
> *potentialities of the energies in your own system.*
> —Joseph Campbell

THE BIG IDEA

The 5 dimensions of teamwork represent the most important elements that impact team member engagement, satisfaction and,
ultimately, performance. The dimensions of communication, conflict management, and engagement exist above the surface in
the iceberg metaphor of conscious awareness. The remaining
two dimensions, purpose, and trust, exist below the surface in the
team's shadow. Interviews for each dimension as well as practical
strategies for enhancing each element are explored.

Introduction

The *5 dimensions of teamwork* represent my attempt to synthesize the most important factors that impact team performance and member satisfaction. Each dimension, *communication, conflict management, engagement, purpose,* and *trust,* represents a critical and unique element of working together in groups. These elements of group dynamics and team performance serve as the switching gears for translating culture into team performance. A higher performing, more dynamic team will score higher in these areas which represent more effective execution in these dimensions. Likewise, a lower performing, less dynamic team (which would be a more detached, dramatic or dependent culture), will score lower in these areas to correspond with less optimal group behavior and team performance.

These five dimensions exist as both norms and artifacts, depending on the dimension. Norms are the unwritten rules of engagement for a team and even though they are not readily visible, they have a tremendous impact on performance. If you think of culture using the analogy of an iceberg, norms are below the surface of the water and, as such, are not readily visible. In the Actualized Teamwork Framework, *purpose* and *trust* are below the surface. On the other hand, artifacts are cultural elements that are more readily visible and occur above the water line. *Communication, conflict management,* and *engagement* (or the external manifestations of these dimensions) are more readily apparent and visible to the team in the emerging group dynamics of a team focused on sharing information, solving problems, making decisions, and capturing emerging opportunities. Figure 9.1 illustrates these five dimensions using the iceberg metaphor.

This chapter is focused on defining and exploring each dimension and includes an interview with a respected business leader. Please note that resources to further improve and enhance these elements of teamwork may be found in the Appendixes, including *The 5 Dimensions of Teamwork Resource Development Guide.* In addition to this guide, a number of other resources are provided in the

Figure 9.1. The 5 dimensions of teamwork

Appendixes that can help improve or enhance these dimensions. For example, the groupthink worksheet helps to resolve group-level conflict, while the Abilene paradox focuses on improving communication.

Dimension 1: Communication

Appreciate everything your associates do for the business. Nothing else can quite substitute for well-chosen, well-timed, sincere words of praise. They're absolutely free and worth a fortune.

—Sam Walton

Communication is the lifeblood of teamwork. Communication has drastically changed in our post-COVID-19 world. Remote work, Zoom meetings, and social media updates have altered and forever changed how and why we communicate with each other. And although the channels have changed, the vital role and importance of communication for effective teamwork and organizational performance has not.

In their 2009 classic *Harvard Business Review* article "A Culture of Candor," authors James O'Toole and Warren Bennis explore the critical importance of transparency and disclosure for team and organizational authenticity and performance. They also acknowledge that the psychological forces that often lead to groupthink, getting on the road to Abilene, or the personal power dynamics that come from holding onto information, make this task very difficult. This section is designed to both define and explore team communication, and to explore ways to enhance the flow of the lifeblood of teamwork (see Figure 9.2).

Figure 9.2. The 5 dimensions of teamwork: Communication

Communication Defined

The degree to which your team communicates openly, candidly, and without hidden agendas.

Before we examine some practical strategies for improving communication, the long-lost art of listening should be reviewed first.

Actively engaging with another team member and listening to their ideas and perspectives, without judgment or a need to defend your position or be right, is essential. So many of us, yours truly included, too often listen to respond (I'm especially talking to my fellow asserters here). If we can slow down and listen for understanding instead of responding, we dramatically change the dynamic of the conversation and, quite often, the outcome of the discussion.

In a team setting, there are some simple steps leaders can take to help improve the quality of communication and discussion. First, open the discussion by defining reality or the current situation *without* adding your opinion or perspective. Ask others first. Actively listen to the responses and, if needed, ask clarifying questions. Try to manage engagement and participation to make sure that everyone, not just the loudest or most assured voice, is heard and valued. Summarize what you heard and then test for agreement.

And, of course, here is where it gets complicated. As we reviewed in Part III Chapters 6 and 7, there are two classic pitfalls in team communication and decision-making: groupthink (the inability to manage team conflict) and the Abilene paradox (the inability to manage team agreement). Take precautions and intentional steps to ensure that your team members don't feel coerced or are not engaging in negative fantasies, so that you are hearing what your teammates truly think and feel. Appendix F provides additional resources to help you navigate these murky waters by shining some light on this team shadow.

As a leader and facilitator, you will need to know when to open the team communication processes broadly with a new or ill-defined challenge (e.g., brainstorming, Appendix D), or when to narrow and close in on a decision or selection (e.g., Nominal Group Technique [NGT], Appendix E). Additional resources in the Appendixes, such as Force Field Analysis, help more visual learners see the problem or challenge (and solution), while also helping team members build ideas and solutions off of each other. Finally, encourage truth-telling, even when it hurts, and transparency. As a leader, if you model admitting your mistakes and having crucial conversations, you will give permission to your teammates to practice these important skills too.

Actualized Teamwork Dimension in Action: Communication
Marlene Hendricks (Marlene Hendricks is the chief customer experience officer at US Auto Trust.)

> Communication is absolutely essential for optimal team performance and member engagement. Members want to contribute and need to understand the broader context in which we are operating, and effective communication is key. At the fundamental level it's how information is transferred to others.
>
> I have found over my career that while that may sound easy, it is actually quite challenging. I learned years ago that when it comes to communication, one size definitely does not fit all. Therefore, I take the time to really get to know my teammates so that I can better understand their style and preferences for communicating effectively, both in receiving information and in providing updates. Years ago I used the Myers-Briggs Type Indicator (MBTI) personality profile to help me identify introverts and extroverts on my team so that I could respond accordingly. More recently I have adopted the Actualized Leader and Team Framework because it provides both a valid assessment of individual style as well as the underlying fear that may be getting in the way. A recent example of this occurred when a direct report was discussing a communication challenge he was having with another leader. Both my direct report and myself are affirmers, and he was working with an asserter. I immediately picked up on his frequent use of the statement "I feel…" and remembered that asserters (and achievers)

will likely and unconsciously discount whatever follows that statement. I was therefore able to coach him on replacing that phrase with "I think. . ." or "Data we've collected suggests that. . ." in order to better speak the language of our asserter colleague.

While there are many barriers to optimal communication, from my perspective there are three that are most reoccurring. First, we have different styles and different approaches and as such have different communication needs. Whether we see it through the lens of the MBTI and introversion versus extroversion, or the actualized leadership profile (ALP) Framework and achievers versus affirmers versus asserters, it can be easy to forget that not everyone receives and processes information like I do. Second, I believe that active listening is very, very hard. We often listen to respond or to win, as opposed to learn and understand. I have found that when I actively engage in the latter, I grow and learn about my colleagues, my organization, and myself, while also building genuine trust with others. And third, organizational structure often gets in the way of optimal communication. Whether there is a matrixed organization with multiple managers, or too many layers of formal hierarchy between the decision maker and where the work actually gets done, recognizing this dynamic helps me decide if issues are a preference or a real problem, and I choose my battles accordingly.

One team communication challenge that I am very much aware of is the mismanaged agreement at the heart of the Abilene paradox. As an affirmer, I go out of my way to make sure that everyone on my team is engaged in our discussion, debates, and dialogue so that we surface issues and concerns and avoid unnecessary trips to Abilene. I use a facilitative approach so that whether introverted or extroverted, affirmer or asserter, individuals feel comfortable participating in our team discussions. Using flipchart paper and individual voting based on a modified NGT has consistently delivered both better decisions and much greater engagement for my teams. I also know that as a leader I often must get out of my fear of rejection leadership shadow to have the difficult conversations that, while sometimes uncomfortable, ultimately help the individual and the team perform at truly exceptional levels.

Dimension 2: Conflict Management

As iron sharpens iron, so one person sharpens another.
—Proverbs 27:17

Even though research studies consistently show that teams and boards produce better decisions when there is constructive conflict and a healthy amount of debate, conflict is still somewhat of a dirty word and taboo topic among and within teams. Leaders, often uncomfortable with the prospect of trying to facilitate group conflict, will often rush to diffuse it with statements like "let's take that conversation offline," or the like, and in doing so, they often inhibit the synergy and enhanced perspective, understanding, and empathy that can come from constructive conflict.

In the actualized team profile (ATP) Framework, we most often see unhealthy conflict and personal attacks in the detached culture that lead to anger and apathy, and often result in groupthink (see Chapter 6). When overt peer pressure is applied to team members to support an option or decision alternative, and when other voices are silenced, it becomes increasingly likely that the team may be a victim of groupthink. It is paramount for leaders to realize that conflict is both natural and potentially very healthy and productive (see Figure 9.3). It often energizes a team and creates greater awareness among

team members which can, in turn, lead to synergy and more optimal decision making. Appendix F is designed to help diagnose and
manage groupthink, while Appendix E is offered as an intervention
tool to help navigate the sometimes stormy waters of team conflict.

Figure 9.3. The 5 dimensions of teamwork: Conflict management

Conflict Management Defined

*The degree to which conflict in your team is recognized and effec-
tively managed in a productive manner.*

In their 2000 *Harvard Business Review* article "How Management
Teams Can Have a Good Fight," authors Kathleen M. Eisenhardt,
Jean L. Kahwajy, and L. J. Bourgeois III outline steps that can facilitate healthy debate and constructive engagement. They make the
point that in order to have a positive outcome and avoid detachment,
teams must minimize interpersonal conflict. They demonstrate how

often team conflict turns into personal attacks that can erode performance and permanently damage relationships. They suggest that focusing on agreed-upon facts, multiplying alternatives and options, and finding common ground and shared goals and objectives help to manage conflict and often difficult conversations in a more productive and less personal way.

As a leader, it is crucial to set the tone and model objectivity, transparency, and empathy toward others. First, focus on your own awareness and understanding of the likely biases that may hinder your objectivity and fairness in team meetings. For example, if you are an asserter then you will likely need to manage confirmation bias which is the tendency to notice and attend to data points that support your position while ignoring or rationalizing contrary information (see Chapters 3–5 for shadow biases by style).

Another common shadow bias that creeps into all three styles is the fundamental attribution error. This common error is when you attribute negative behavior of others to their personality or character, while attributing your own shortcomings to situational factors. For example, you may attribute a teammate arriving late to a meeting as a sign of disrespect to you or apathy for the situation. However, if you are late for a meeting you a more likely to blame a last minute crisis or fire that couldn't wait to justify your own tardiness. Becoming hyperaware of these common shadow biases can go a very long way in helping leaders facilitate fairly.

Other effective strategies for effectively managing conflict include actively listening to all views, perspectives, and suggestions, especially the ones you may not agree with from the outset. Be constructive in your feedback, always focusing on the idea or proposed solution and not the individual. Finally, set the example for collegial candor by being honest, frank, and sincere in your communications with others. Being direct and candid with your team will help ensure that there are no hidden agendas—or perceptions of hidden agendas—which is critical for building and maintaining trust.

Actualized Teamwork Dimension in Action: Conflict Management
Kathie Patterson (Kathie Patterson serves as the chief human
resources officer at Ally Financial.)

Managing conflict is a critical part of leading teams
effectively. Unfortunately, there is a gap between the
frequent need to engage in healthy debate and conflict
resolution, and the actual skill sets that many professionals bring to the team. Moreover, many individuals often
lack the confidence to engage in rigorous discussion
and dialogue with their teammates, which often creates
a negatively charged emotional setting that can lead to
outright avoidance.

Before discussing team-level conflict specifically,
I would like to highlight some strategies for managing
conflict that have served me well over the years, whether
the conflict was occurring at the personal (individual) or
interpersonal (team) level. First, and perhaps most importantly, it is crucial for the party to be heard. I try very
hard to actively listen to each party so that they know
they've been heard. This process requires psychological
safety. And while leaders must make sure that their teammates feel heard, they must also ensure that they do not
feel shame, judgment, or fear of retribution. Second, I
intentionally ask the individual, "What is the other party
saying and feeling about you and or the situation?" I have
found that this question often helps expand a person's
perspective and, in doing so, creates greater empathy for
the other party. Third, I ask them, "What is the specific
outcome you are seeking in this resolution?" Sometimes
the outcome is more related to the relationship, while
other times it may be more performance or project specific. When the desired outcome is more relational, I ask
them if the conflict is a single episode, or if there is a

pattern of behavior that needs to be addressed. Finally, I ask them to reflect on what the actual trigger is that has been activated. Oftentimes, especially when dealing with very strong emotions, the individual's reaction may be out of proportion to the actual event. In this case, I encourage the individual to explore the deeper meaning of what internal mechanism or unresolved issue may have created such a strong reaction.

At the team level, managing conflict is a facilitation challenge because the unit of analysis is greater. As an affirmer I am acutely aware of the tendency to smooth over surface-level or seemingly minor microtransgressions. However, it has been my experience that small conflicts ignored or left unresolved usually lead to big blowups at the team level. Leaders must have both the insight to identify conflict, sometimes residing beneath the surface, and the courage to call it out openly. That white elephant in the room will only grow in size if it is not addressed quickly and openly. Having said that, it is important to address it in a non-judgmental manner, without blame. To that end, I will often say, "I sense there are opposing views on this issue" or "I am getting the sense that some of you do not feel heard." Framing the conflict identification in this manner helps to both depersonalize and de-escalate an emotionally charged environment. In my area, talent planning meetings often have a super-charged emotional climate where leaders are strongly advocating for their direct reports. Oftentimes, their close working relationships with certain individuals may cloud their objectivity. Other teammates may not share their perspective on performance or potential. In these kinds of meetings, I have found that it is productive to call a "5 Minute Pause" timeout to allow folks to collectively exhale and reset.

Finally, I think it is incumbent on everyone to spend time in personal reflection. Increasing our self-awareness, specifically with regard to our own personal triggers and why we have such strong reactions to certain people, will help manage those situations more effectively. Simply asking yourself the following questions will help deepen personal reflection: "What worked well today?" "What did I accomplish?" What didn't work well?" "What can I change or do differently tomorrow?" Reflection seems to come more naturally for affirmers. But I have found that if we want to grow and develop, we have to commit to an action plan to put our insights to work. Closing the reflection loop with changes in behavior helps us to stop overthinking and to start realizing our full potential.

Dimension 3: Engagement

When people are financially invested, they want to return. When people are emotionally invested, they want to contribute.

—Simon Sinek

There is quite a history when it comes to employee engagement and participation. Decades ago, the term satisfaction was used to describe the degree to which people felt connected to their work and fully engaged in their team's efforts. In fact, one of my graduate school mentors, the late Dr. Erik Winslow, had been a doctoral student under Frederick Herzberg, whose two-factor theory of motivation and workplace satisfaction is arguably the most influential still to this day. Herzberg's classic *Harvard Business Review* article "One More Time: How Do You Motivate Employees?" is an all-time bestseller.

Today, there is tremendous emphasis placed on employee engagement. From the Gallup Q12 surveys to numerous business and research articles, we are becoming more adept at enhancing and increasing this subtle yet incredibly important factor of individual and team performance. The evidence is overwhelming: engaged employees are more productive, more satisfied (and, as a result, greater ambassadors for the organization), less burned out, and more likely to stay longer. Figure 9.4 illustrates how engagement exists just at the waterline of team culture, and while it is technically not visible, it is easily deduced from patterns (or lack thereof) of communication and team member interactions.

Figure 9.4. The 5 dimensions of teamwork: Engagement

Engagement Defined

The degree to which each team member is engaged and actively participates in meetings and takes responsibility for achieving your team's goals.

Given the new normal of remote work in our post-COVID-19 environment today, engagement has become an extremely critical factor for leaders to consider and prioritize. While some companies have adopted a standard "must be in the office for three days a work, work remote two day" approach, other organizations are taking a more nuanced look at this challenge in an effort to improve engagement, retention, and ultimately, recruitment. In her *Harvard Business Review* article "Manage Your Team's Collective Time" (2014), Leslie Perlow cites multiple studies and applied research efforts demonstrating the impact of delegation, team empowerment, and control on improved employee engagement. For example, scheduling *enhanced* or *predictable* workdays—days when all hands are expected to be on deck—is an effective way to not only ensure greater equity, but also to realize the benefits of having the critical mass of most employees in the office. Not only does this approach yield greater productivity and enhanced engagement, it also creates an opportunity for building stronger workplace and team culture as members have more informal time together, either over morning coffees or after-work dinner and drinks.

Although engagement can be a bit nebulous because it attempts to operationalize how someone feels, there are four agreed-upon areas that engagement includes:

» Felt commitment to the organization,
» Identification with the organization's purpose,
» Felt satisfaction with their job, and
» Felt energy with their specific role.

In their *Harvard Business Review* article "How Companies Can Improve Employee Engagement Right Now" (2021), authors Daniel Stein, Nick Hobson, Jon M. Jachimowicz, and Ashley Whillans offer a number of checklist items that managers can discuss with team members to help ensure alignment on this crucial element. Their suggestions follow:

» **Connect employees to what they care about**. Consider developing a team mission or purpose statement (see Appendix C) that connects individual efforts with overall organizational strategy. Also, make sure that your team members have time to participate in affinity group interest meetings and have paid time off for volunteer opportunities that are near and dear to their hearts.

» **Make the workload less stressful and more fun.** Create opportunities for your team members to creatively flex their work tasks and priorities with other team members, and whenever possible, grant as much autonomy to your team members as possible (i.e., less directive, more actualized).

» **Create time affluence.** Consider ways to reward your team members (especially mothers) with additional time off, and whenever possible, partner with third-party vendors who can come onsite to increase accessibility and convenience for your team. Also, consider implementing new norms (or even technological tools) that discourage after-hour emails so that there is dedicated time off.

Actualized Teamwork Dimension in Action: Engagement
Jonathan S. Halkyard (Jonathan S. Halkyard serves as the chief financial officer of Metro-Goldwyn-Mayer [MGM] Resorts International.)

Creating and sustaining team engagement is essential for both high levels of performance and high levels of team member satisfaction. This effort requires time, and while it isn't created overnight, it is well worth that investment.

In order to effectively create this type of team culture, I engage in a facilitative approach to leadership that orchestrates learning and development—both mine and the team's. While I have significant experience in the finance arena, I realize I am not a subject matter expert in every function and I try to create an environment where the expert can educate the entire team, including me.

I have discovered an interesting paradox as it relates to team engagement: balancing the tension between the need for internal trust and vulnerability with the external need for performance and execution. I maintain extremely high expectations for performance, and there are certain functions where we must be perfect every single time. And there are other instances when we can afford to be creative and try something new, knowing we might not succeed. For example, in our business and with our brand, the guest's room upon arrival must always be perfect—there is no excuse for anything less than perfection. We have to deliver excellence on this front every single time. However, trying a new innovative restaurant concept that may or may not succeed is usually worth the risk. Even when we fail there is tremendous learning that occurs, arguably more than when we succeed.

So, with that paradox of team engagement in mind, here are my suggestions for leaders who want to create and sustain higher levels of member engagement:

» **Create vulnerability and trust**: Facilitate curious and engaged team learning, not just learning from me but, more importantly, learning from each other. Team members who are willing to be vulnerable are more likely to ask for help or quickly admit a mistake.

» **Listen first, speak last**. I've realized that sometimes the best way for me to add value is to subtract my initial reaction and speak toward the end of the meeting. This approach allows me to consider the expertise and perspectives of my teammates before moving to a decision.

» **Engage with others on multiple levels**. Everything we do in our industry is to support our front-line workers. To that end, having lunch in our cafeteria when I can (usually two or three times a week) allows me to get to know team members across the entire organization while enhancing the way others (often younger professionals) experience me.

» **Treat everyone on my team fairly**. It is important that I reserve the same amount of bandwidth for all of my teammates. Even though there may be certain personalities or organizational functions that I am more drawn to, it is imperative that I am balanced and equitable in my approach to working with my direct reports.

» **Look for humor and laugh**. I have learned the importance of humor in sustaining high levels of team engagement. Humor allows all to relax and connect in a more authentic way, and it is also just a more fun way to work!

How do I know when these efforts are working? I know we have a high level of engagement when my teammates in finance (either direct reports or someone several layers down in the organization) come into my office with their own unique insights and ideas for solving problems. When team members feel comfortable enough to share off-the-wall ideas and creative suggestions for improvements, we all perform at our highest levels.

Dimension 4: Purpose

Life is never made unbearable by circumstances,
but only by lack of meaning and purpose.
—Viktor Frankl

In their *Harvard Business Review* article entitled "Creating a Purpose-Driven Organization," Robert E. Quinn and Anjan V. Thakor (2018) remind us that organizations, much like individuals, discover their true purpose during challenging times. An organization's true essence and culture are revealed by what leaders do, and don't do, during difficult times. Joseph Campbell (2008) once said,

"We must be willing to let go of the life we've planned to have the life that is waiting for us." That's a good first step, and one that is frankly easier and more natural to do during challenging and difficult times when the old way no longer works. Organizations, teams, and individuals must be willing to let go of what you think you should be, or what someone told you that you should be, so that you can become who you are intended to be.

Purpose Defined

The degree to which your team has a sense of meaning and purpose, and an understanding of how decisions and actions impact the larger goals and objectives of the organization.

In the 5 dimensions of teamwork, *purpose* is the first dimension that exists primarily below the waterline of conscious awareness and, as such, resides in the team's collective shadow. It is within this realm of teamwork that groups ponder questions of *how?* and *why?* as they relate to working together. Figure 9.5 illustrates the *purpose* dimension.

When it comes to discovering your team's purpose, there is a critical link between individual purpose and organizational purpose that must be explicitly made and communicated. *Team purpose* is the linking pin between individual meaning and organizational mission (see Figure 9.6), and in order to authentically resonate and connect with team members, it must be calibrated in such a way that it provides a meaningful conduit between individual purpose and the overall mission and purpose of the organization.

A team's purpose should be grounded on the collective individual purpose statements of its members while also cascading up to connect to the broader goals, objectives, and mission of the organization. A team purpose statement that does not account for one or the other of these dimensions is not sustainable and will ultimately give way. Appendix C provides the *Team Purpose Worksheet*

Figure 9.5. The 5 dimensions of teamwork: Purpose

Figure 9.6. Team purpose

to help craft this crucial statement for optimizing performance and calibrating difficult team decisions that deal with ambiguity or right versus right alternatives, what Harvard Business Professor Joseph Badaracco (1997) refers to as "defining moments."

Jonathan Knowles, B. Tom Hunsaker, Hannah Grove, and Alison James (2022) remind us that everyone can't save the world, and organizational and team purpose can occur on three distinct levels: competence, cause and culture. In their *Harvard Business Review* article "What Is the Purpose of Your Purpose?", the authors refer to these three areas as the "senses of purpose," which follow:

» **Competence**: The function that our product serves.
» **Cause**: The social good to which we aspire.
» **Culture**: The intent with which we run the business.

This classification is especially useful for teams who may be struggling to understand what working together in their roles on a daily basis, sometimes very far upstream from the final product or service provided by the organization, has to do with purpose. For example, a technology team may have difficulty understanding how they are directly impacting the environment for good, but they can very often connect their efforts with the great good (competence) or the larger system (culture) in which they operate.

The *Team Purpose Worksheet* assumes that you have discovered your unique individual purpose. Quite often, a leap of faith is required to fully embrace your purpose as you must be willing to embrace the fear that is standing between your current position and your potential. Deciding to live life with purpose often requires changes, some small and some drastic. Making these changes will likely require you to get out of your comfort zone, and to face your fears and insecurities. As transcendental poet Ralph Waldo Emerson (2020) framed it, "God will not have his work made manifest by cowards . . . always do what you are afraid to do. Do the thing you fear, and the death of fear is certain."

Are you living and leading on purpose, or is your purpose waiting to be discovered and actualized? What do you need to let go of for your purpose to find you? What fear must you be willing to face in order to pursue your destiny? Finally, what impact will you have had on the world when, at the very end, you can respond: "Yes, I lived my life on purpose."

Actualized Teamwork Dimension in Action: Purpose
Brian Savoy (Brian Savoy serves as executive vice president and chief financial officer [CFO] of Duke Energy.)

Purpose drives excellence and it creates resiliency and persistence. Exploring and identifying purpose at a personal level is crucial for identifying my *why* to the many complex and often competing demands in life. Likewise, exploring and aligning on team and organizational purpose is crucial for not only providing meaning and a broader collective context for our individual acts, but it also provides a common language and framework for bringing together a diverse array of teammates for accomplishing a common goal.

On a personal level, purpose provides greater passion and resiliency for working on the most complex challenges and important issues I'm facing. Years ago, my pastor discussed purpose and how it must connect to the most important people in our lives. I gave that a lot of thought and consideration, and developed the following personal goals as they relate to my personal purpose in life:

» Be a husband worth respecting.
» Be a father worth imitating.
» Be a leader worth following.

On a professional level, especially as it relates to my teammates, I have discovered that my purpose is to help unlock the potential of others. I see my role as helping to facilitate my teammates' realization of their highest potential through asking good questions and providing the necessary support to help them be all they can be.

Purpose at the collective level is crucial for a number of reasons. First, it provides a greater context for understanding and connecting the why of our individual acts to a greater good. Second, it inspires higher levels of performance from team members. Third, it infuses in others greater resiliency and persistence to go the extra mile for our customers and teammates. And finally, it provides a common language and framework for each team member to feel a unique connection to a larger group. For example, years ago I served the company as the chief information officer (CIO). In this role, I had to bridge the gap that sometimes existed between traditional information technology (IT) and digital. I quickly realized that even though the two groups were often using different words (e.g., IT talked about *reliability* and *up-time* while digital used words like *agility* and *outcomes*, etc.) they were essentially saying the same thing. Exploring and clarifying our team purpose helped us all connect on the same overarching goals and objectives and, in doing so, made us more effective in our roles.

In my current role as CFO, I am responsible for both finance and strategy within the company and, in many ways, face a similar challenge. And again, I have found that exploring and aligning on a broader team purpose has allowed us to more effectively connect the often shorter-term measurable goals of finance with the often more conceptual longer-term objectives of strategy.

Irrespective of my role with Duke Energy, we are all responsible for a climate strategy that moves us to a net-zero carbon emissions future. Realizing this outcome will help make our business more sustainable and our world a little better for future generations to come. On a very deep level, this purpose energizes and drives all of us.

Dimension 5: Trust

*Without trust we don't truly collaborate, we coordinate. It
is trust that transforms a group of people into a team.*

—Stephen Covey

Trust is the currency of leadership and teamwork. When teammates trust each other, optimal performance, innovation, and
synergistic outcomes become the norm. The process of collective
realization of group potential—*team-actualization*—can occur
only when members trust enough to be vulnerable, transparent,
and candid. To be clear, I am not using trust in the sense of being
trustworthy, which has more to do with leadership characteristics such as authenticity and integrity and is a component of the
broader sense of trust.

In a 2017 *Harvard Business Review* article, author Paul Zak
examined the neuroscience of trust and found that high-trust teams
report 74 percent less stress than low-trust teams. Moreover, trust
is not only correlated with a sense of purpose, it also creates joy
at work. As a result, trust is foundational engagement, productivity, and satisfaction. From an actualized teamwork perspective, let's
define the dimension of trust and explore ways to build and enhance
it at work.

Trust Defined

*The degree to which team members trust each other and their
leader, act in the best interest of the group, maintain confidential-
ity, and speak and act with integrity.*

It has often been said that trust is the most precious gift we give to
another person, and once it is destroyed it is very difficult to rees-
tablish. Yes, it can be rebuilt, but the analogy of a crumpled piece of
paper is perhaps most helpful: you can straighten the sheet back out

again over time, but even when it's flat, it's never quite the same. Figure 9.7 illustrates the *trust* dimension.

So, what does all of this mean for leading teams? Recently, a group of executives was asked to list the three people they trusted the most. After parents, they typically mentioned siblings and spouses, with an occasional best friend. In this exercise, no one named their boss. However, when this same group was asked to list the three people who had the greatest impact on their happiness, boss was listed in every instance. That's a very telling finding and chances are you are the boss for someone. How much impact do you have on your team's happiness and satisfaction? And do they trust you?

There are several things you can do to help build, sustain, and enhance trust in your team. First, as Hugh McColl stated in my last book *Actualized Leadership*, you have to start with an authentic concern and caring for others. As he stated, it cannot be faked: "you have to actually care about your teammates." Second, being consistent, transparent, and fair in the way you work with others is what team members can observe and will believe. Your intentions,

Figure 9.7. The 5 dimensions of teamwork: Trust

however well-intentioned, cannot be observed or accounted for. Finally, the especially polarizing world we live in today can be a unique challenge to establishing trust. In their *Harvard Business Review* article "Managing a Polarized Workforce: How to Foster Debate and Promote Trust," authors Julia A. Minson and Francesca Gino explore how leaders can embrace deep divides and polarization by fostering debate, discussion, and yes, even disagreement. Their findings suggest that by acknowledging the other party's position and perspective and by emphasizing areas of agreement, leaders are much more effective in navigating divisions and disagreements in teams and, in doing so, more successful in building genuine and authentic trust among the team.

Actualized Teamwork Dimension in Action: Trust

James R. Jordan (James R. Jordan serves as the interim president and chief operating officer of the Charlotte Hornets.)

> Behavior builds trust. Words by themselves do not build trust. And when what we say is not aligned with what we do, leaders destroy trust.
>
> Before joining the Charlotte Hornets, I served in the US Army as an airborne soldier. During my thirty-one years of service, I held leadership positions and ranks with increasing responsibility. Candidly, my experiences and lessons learned as a soldier inform the business leader I am today. Everything I know about building trust in group settings comes from my military experience.
>
> First, people watch what you do, not what you say. If your words and actions don't match, people will always believe the behavior. If you want to build trust, you must consistently make sure that what you say matches what you do. This can't be some of the time or even most of the time. The alignment between your words and your actions must be consistent all the time.

Second, to build trust, leaders must be selfless. I always strive to make the meeting about the members of the team, not myself. This approach is key to helping individuals and teams perform at their best. When you approach leading teams from a selfless perspective, you can get your ego out of the way and really listen and learn from others. The military taught me not only to ask good questions, but also to listen carefully to the answers that follow. Oftentimes, in my meetings, I will do very little or no talking. Instead, I allow my teammates to discuss and clarify issues and challenges, often speaking up only to call the meeting to a close when we agree on our mission. Allowing team members to take ownership is important.

Third, building trust absolutely requires that you grant both accountability and forgiveness for mistakes. People who are afraid to make mistakes will never give you their very best. Mistakes are tremendous learning opportunities and teammates who are afraid to make mistakes limit not only their learning, they also limit their performance and that of the entire organization.

Finally, candor and transparency are key. Everybody on the team must know what is really going on so that we can focus on the reality of our challenges and opportunities. Sugar-coating the truth or avoiding a difficult conversation only makes things worse. Leadership requires the courage to speak the truth and the faith that your team will be better for it.

What's Next

This chapter introduced and explored the 5 dimensions of teamwork. Each dimension was defined and illustrated and supplemented with an interview from a respected business leader. Chapter 10 links these dimensions to group dynamics and provides a process for transforming team culture and, in the process, increasing member engagement, improving communication, and optimizing team performance. Specific attention is paid to each of the three shadow cultures—detached, dramatic, and dependent—with specific strategies and suggestions offered for transforming each unique culture to a more dynamic level.

Chapter 10
Transforming Team Culture

What's in this Chapter?

» The Tension Between Leadership and Teamwork
» Strategic Orientation and Intuition
» Developing Team Culture
» The Team Transformation Cycle
» Putting It All Together

THE BIG IDEA

Transforming team culture to a more dynamic state is examined in this chapter. Specific strategies related to each unique culture, as well as emerging best practices, are explored as practical tools and applications that can have immediate, positive impacts on team performance. The chapter closes with a review of the team transformation cycle, a group-level process of shadow dialogue and integration that is foundational for creating lasting, sustainable, positive change in team settings.

Transforming team culture is a process and while crucial insights often occur in an instant, lasting change occurs over a period of sustained and intentional efforts designed to improve and enhance leader and team member interaction and performance. Long-standing traditions within the team, the legacy and shadow of the team's former leader, and the larger organizational culture in which your team is operating can be forces that inhibit growth and transformation. These challenges can be met, however, and while a one-day team development session may not create lasting results, I have facilitated numerous sessions where the shift in the culture could be felt as the transformation process started.

The Tension Between Leadership and Teamwork

Psychologists, sociologists, political scientists, and many other researchers from diverse fields have long acknowledged the inherent tension between individuality and group life. Whether we are dealing with peer pressure, social loafing, or the mob mentality, there seems to be a constant push-and-pull between individual goals and the will of the group. Carl Jung remarked that whenever one hundred clever individuals join a group, "one big nincompoop" is the result. And these observations don't apply just to social experiments in labs and classroom settings, or to our polarized political climate today. This tension, on some level, exists in every interaction between a leader and their team. And this tension also exists between the individual members of the team and the group as a whole. A ubiquitous example of this tension in organizational life is the micromanaging leader. These individuals, rushed to meet deadlines or worried about failures, micromanage a team on deliverables to the point where they essentially do all of the work. This tendency to micromanage is an outcome of this tension between the individual and the team—the tension to get results—which is often at the expense of delegation and the team member development that often accompanies it. In the short term or in isolated examples, the process of micromanaging can actually work and lead to a productive outcome. However, in the long run, it is the least useful and most destructive approach to building a dynamic culture and a high performing team. The micromanaging tendency, readily apparent in all three styles but most closely associated with achievers, creates the lowest performing culture (detached) and over time can lead to total failure or attrition of highly capable individual members.

Having been engaged in leader, team, and organization development for thirty years, I can unequivocally state that transformation and lasting development—both for the leader and team—must occur in concert together. As CaSondra Devine points out in this book's introduction, individual wounding occurs in community, and so do healing and transformation. In other words, we are both wounded and healed in community. Likewise, leaders transform themselves in the context of their team, while lasting team development and transformation must occur in the context of a developing leader.

I cannot count the number of times managers have asked me—either explicitly or implicitly—to fix them. "Them" being their team. And almost always the leader asking for this fix was an asserter. And you guessed it, the team culture was dependent. Ironically part of the issue adversely impacting team performance, sometimes all the issue, is the leader. I came to realize that not only were these "fix them" team building sessions ineffective, they were ultimately counterproductive. In other words, a session designed at the team level only, without the leader's total buy-in and full participation, actually makes things worse. As I matured on my professional journey this dynamic became more clear to me. Over the last decade or so, when faced with this dilemma, I tell the prospective client my "F in Life" story (see Chapter 1 in *Actualized Leadership*) or ask them to watch my TED Talk "The Power of Self Awareness." Essentially, I tell the leader that I also wanted the other party (i.e., my ex-wife) to be remedied, and some sympathy along the way would be appreciated too. As this story unfolds, they begin to see themselves in my role as the instigator of creating the dysfunction of dependency. Usually at some point, the potential client will ask me something along the lines of "so, you're giving me an 'F' in life?" When I reply "yes," they either chuckle and engage my firm, or bristle and show me the door. Either outcome is preferable to standing up in front of a group of individuals and asking them to engage in, and commit to, a process that I know without the buy-in and commitment from the leader, will fail. Actually, things will be worse when the realization sets in that the leader sees them as broken. To create lasting and sustainable positive change to support a team's transformational journey, we must recognize and appreciate the symbiotic relationship between leader and team, and work together in identifying, acknowledging, and integrating the leadership and team shadows that are preventing optimal performance or team-actualization.

Figure 10.1 illustrates the *actualized performance cycle*, first introduced in my book *Actualized Leadership: Meeting Your Shadow & Maximizing Your Potential*. While previous chapters have examined the different actualized performance and different actualized leadership profile (ALP) leader styles on the dimensions of *orientation* (strategic vs. tactical) and *problem-solving* (logical vs. intuitive), the figure more demonstrably illustrates that more *actualized leaders* are less directive.

Let me state that again, for the record: more self-actualized leaders are less directive. And the result of a less directive approach is a more dynamic (i.e., actualized) team culture and higher levels

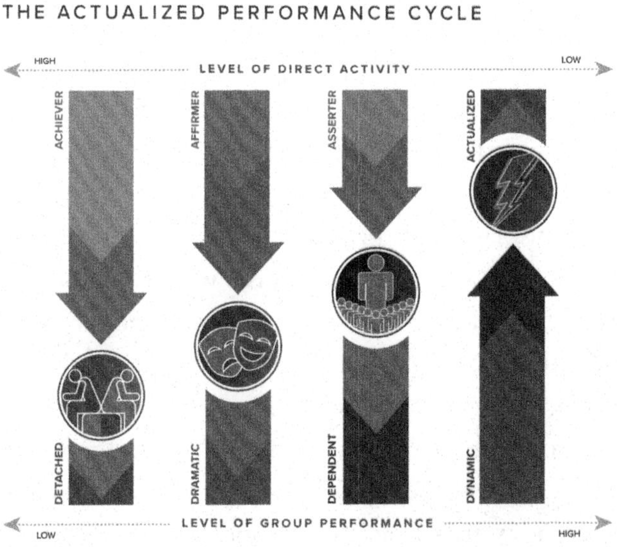

THE ACTUALIZED PERFORMANCE CYCLE

Figure 10.1. The actualized performance cycle

of team performance and member engagement. Before examining specific methods for developing and transforming teams by specific culture, it would be all for nothing if we did not address the crucial first step: leader development. If the team is going to develop into a more dynamic state, the leader must become less directive. Moreover, directly correlated to becoming less directive is the need for leaders to become both more strategic and more intuitive. When related back to ALP style, there is a development plan that typically emerges. Asserters, who tend to be more strategic, often need to hone in on their intuition and their interpersonal relations with their team members. Affirmers, who tend to be more intuitive, often need to develop a more strategic orientation with a greater emphasis on results and performance. Finally, achievers often need to develop both their strategic orientation and their intuition in order to become less directive, delegating more to the team and focusing on bigger picture and more strategic issues and opportunities.

Strategic Orientation and Intuition

Perhaps the most challenging aspect of leader development is the act of becoming less directive. For many leaders, this change requires intentional focus, trusting others, and delegating important tasks and projects. For leaders who fear failure (achievers) and betrayal (asserters) this act is paramount to a leap of faith and in many ways, counters the very essence of what past success depended on: tactical execution and control. And I know, I can almost see your eyes rolling now as you think to yourself "my situation is different because of. . ." If you want another perspective, I highly recommend Marshall Goldsmith's bestseller *What Got You Here Won't Get You There* where he examines this very dynamic and the inherent difficulty in moving from a contributor or controller mindset to more of a leader mindset. Essentially, his decades of research suggest that the higher up you go in an organization, it's behavioral problems, not technical expertise, that separate average leaders from exceptional ones. Superior, sustainable results come from practicing essential behaviors like saying thank you, active listening, owning and apologizing for mistakes, and most importantly, delegating to others. In other words, the first step on this journey of team transformation is being less directive as the leader.

In the *Harvard Business Review* article (2023) "The Leadership Odyssey," authors Herminia Ibarra, Claudius A. Hildebrand, and Sabine Vinck explore the need for emerging leaders to become less directive and more empowering. In this article they describe this transformative process as occurring in three unique stages: departure, voyage, and return. In the departure phase individuals realize there is a need for change. This realization is often the result of suboptimal results, 360-degree feedback, or a manager or mentor's observation that reinforces the distinction between the current state (doing too much), the desired state (leading more strategically), and the need for an intentional shift.

The second phase is the voyage, and it is within this phase where leaders must let go of their old habits and ways of managing and embrace a new way of collaborating. Subtle yet powerful changes in this phase include listening instead of directing, asking instead of telling, and encouraging instead of controlling. Painful, sometimes excruciating vulnerability may be experienced during this time as tried-and-true approaches and tactics are retired, and a new way of working and leading begins to emerge.

The final phase, the return, occurs when the new insights, self-discoveries, and key learnings become internalized, and as a result, the new leadership style (more actualized) and approach for working with others takes root. Although the journey is not over, the former style is permanently retired and a less directive, more empowering, style emerges and is sustained. A key element of the return phase is a newfound appreciation for personal reflection and learning, and these newly enhanced practices help to reinforce a more actualized approach to working with others.

In addition to a more actualized approach being less directive and more empowering, there are two other specific areas for leader development that directly impact team culture and performance. These areas are intuition and strategic orientation, and Figure 2.4 illustrates how actualized leaders are both more strategic and less tactical, while also balancing logic with intuition. Taken together, more strategic and more intuitive, the actualized approach to leading others becomes less directive.

Developing Your Intuition

Let's face it: most of the time we are rewarded for rational, left-brain thinking in our professional lives. Data analytics, logical reasoning, and rational problem solving not only rule our professional lives, but also carry a very strong preference in Western society as a whole. But what about the right side of the brain—intuition? Carl Jung's work is the basis for the Myers-Briggs Type Indicator (MBTI) or personality test, and in his framework intuition is the counterpart to sensing and refers to what data you attend to and how you notice it. Sensors use their five senses and are primarily data driven. Intuitives use their sixth sense or gut and are primarily pattern driven. The reality is that leaders need both a careful analysis of the data coupled with a gut check or feel for the decision at hand and a willingness to trust that feeling.

Studies have indicated that the vast majority of Fortune 500 chief executive officers (CEOs) (85 percent) say that intuition is key to their decision making. A classic *Harvard Business Review* article (2001) by Alden M. Hayashi profiles how former Chrysler President Bob Lutz's intuition led to the wildly successful design and launch of the Dodge Viper, which single-handedly changed the public's perception of Chrysler in the 1990s. Retired Bank of America Chairman and CEO Hugh McColl once told my Master of Business Administration (MBA) class that every major decision he made was based on his gut feel. Even healthcare researchers have found that the most effective and efficient American dentists allow their intuition to inform their most complex and time-sensitive decisions. And in the Actualized Leadership Framework, actualized leaders are both more strategic and more intuitive.

So, what exactly is intuition? Intuition is a form of unconscious (i.e., resides in the shadow), non-verbal, and non-linear thinking that allows us to make instinctive decisions and judgments. Often described as a gut feeling, intuition is built on prior experiences and patterns of behavior. Although certainly not infallible and prone to subjective bias, intuition has a number of advantages and benefits, which include the following:

» **Speed** in fast-paced and ever-changing environments.
» **Easy to use** in the sense that it occurs at the unconscious level and doesn't require expertise or training.
» **Flexibility** that allows leaders to adapt more quickly to novel situations or changing circumstances.
» **Openness** to new ideas or experiences by expanding your sense of emerging patterns and letting go of limiting patterns of a purely rational or logical approach.
» **Caution!** Intuition allows you to sense when things may be off in a team meeting or with a customer, or when your gut may be telling you to steer clear of a proposal.

Based on the examples of intuitive decision making and the potential benefits, let's explore some strategies for becoming a more intuitive leader. Several suggestions are listed here for your consideration:

» **Validate intuition with data.** Perhaps the best way to validate the power of intuitive decision making is to start by coupling it with data and information. Intuition can be enhanced by combining it with data and logical analyses. Combining the flexibility of intuition with the rigor of data enables leaders to make more informed decisions.
» **Trust your expertise and your gut.** Expertise and experience help intuition become more reliable and valid, but you

must attend to both. Trusting yourself and your experience, which includes formal expertise and informal hunches, allows you to combine the two for a more holistic approach to decision making.

» **Reflect on past experiences.** Looking back on past experiences helps us identify patterns and connections previously overlooked. In turn, this new recognition can help us develop a deeper understanding of causal patterns and underlying relationships.

» **Practice mindful reflection.** Much like the stabilizing internalization process for becoming a less directive leader, mindful reflection reinforces the validity of intuition. Reflection helps you to better connect to the power contained in the subconscious (shadow) which in turn helps you identify both repeatable patterns and your personal biases in order to make better decisions.

In summary, enhancing intuition is a daily process that requires self-awareness, the courage to practice (and sometimes suspend) disbelief and reflection. Practicing these recommended steps, as well as asking your teammates how they feel about a certain decision point, will better enable you to tap into the power of intuition while calibrating your subjective hunches and gut feelings with objective data and rational logic.

Enhancing Your Strategic Orientation

In full transparency I am approaching this section of the book with more than a little fear and trembling. You see, I am a product of the School of Business and Public Management at George Washington University (2002) and studied under the late Dr. Jerry Harvey and the late Dr. Elliott Jaques. Dr. Harvey is frequently cited in this book, but Dr. Jaques, who was mentioned in Part 1, may not be as familiar. His contributions, however, mostly likely are. He was the first researcher to use the term *corporate culture* in 1951, and he coined the phrase *mid-life crisis* in his 1965 article "Death and the Mid-Life Crisis."

I feel it would be remiss of me to not at least acknowledge Jaques' work in the area of strategic orientation and to condense his research findings into one statement: strategic orientation, insofar as it relates to managing complexity and ambiguity, is an innate cognitive ability that cannot be enhanced. But Jaques went even further and defined leadership as directly correlated to one's level of cognitive capability or capacity. And to reinforce my previous point, one's ability was innate: that is, set at birth. No amount of experience or formal education would allow a Level 2 leader to effectively perform Level 3 (or higher) work. Just to play this out, Jaques stated that any and all training and development activities aimed at leadership development, as well as any formal educational programs promising improved leadership, were a waste of time and money. As you imagine, he was not very popular on the leadership development circuit.

To be sure, while I do think there is some merit in Jaques' work, I also think there are some critical holes in his theory. He stated in class that we must "assume one leaves their negative psychopathology at home" when they enter a formal organizational setting. Have you ever worked with anyone who left their emotions at home? Me neither. As a result, I think his theory, while useful in many ways, fails to offer the comprehensive framework he intended because he completely discounted emotions and the impact they have on performance. Today we refer to emotional intelligence or soft skills as not only important skills for working with others, but as crucial the higher up you go in an organization.

As such, I do believe that exploring the importance of developing a more strategic orientation and, more importantly, embracing strategies and suggestions for helping you think more strategically, is a worthwhile exercise in leader development. And for hundreds and hundreds of clients and MBA students I worked with over the years who have lamented that they "didn't have time to be strategic," the prior section on directing less and delegating more should open up a vista and some headspace for them to engage in this process.

First, let me try to better define an admittedly vague assertion that to become a more actualized leader you need to think more strategically. Essentially, being more strategic means shifting your time and energy away from tactical execution (implementation) and into longer-term, big picture planning (conceptualization). This shift is crucial to support your leadership and team's journey, and it can also be a bit daunting.

Developing a more strategic mindset is really about enhancing a number of support skills to help you conceptualize and communicate a future desired state, and then to inspire and motivate your team to move toward the long-term goals and objectives. In the *Harvard Business Review* article (2020) "What Are Strategic Thinking Skills?" author Tim Stobierski identifies both the components of a strategic mindset and the specific steps leaders can take to develop these skills. Stobierski states that there are four crucial skills necessary to be an effective strategic thinker:

» **Analytical skills**: The ability to critically assess both external markets and internal capabilities is key in helping to formulate both an inspiring desired future state, and an objective gap analysis that considers an accurate current state.

» **Communication skills**: The ability to clearly and concisely communicate what can be complex and often competing values to your various stakeholder groups to build support and inspire behavior.

» **Problem-solving skills**: The ability to identify and understand the root causes of underlying problems and challenges, as well as potential strategic imperatives and solutions to address said problems.

» **Management skills**: The ability to put all of these skills together from analysis to implementation to build and sustain a guiding coalition and the focus to successfully direct productive human behavior.

It is important to examine specific actions you can take to cultivate a more strategic mindset. There are a number of fairly simple yet powerful and effective activities that you and your team can engage in that will help broaden your perspective, align tactical behaviors with long-term objectives, and increase overall engagement and commitment to the endeavor at hand. While the list here is by no means exhaustive, it provides a good starting point to becoming a more strategic leader.

» **Understand your organization's strategy and how your team supports it.** You and your team's behavior must align with the overall strategy of your organization, and this sort of cascading effect helps to ensure that your efforts will create synergies and momentum throughout the entire organization.

» **Start with *why*.** Strategy involves questions of *why* which often relate to purpose and even meaning. Execution and implementation are more concerned with questions of *how* and *when*, so be sure you can understand and answer questions of *why*.

» **Ask strategic questions.** The process of simply asking more broad, long-term questions not only helps to provide additional information and context on a strategic level, it also shifts your mindset and attention to thinking in terms of big picture and longer-term.

» **Discuss your plan with others and ask for critical reactions.** Talking with others, both inside and outside your team and organization, helps to calibrate your thinking and often provides crucial insight into faulty assumptions that need to be reassessed before moving forward.

» **Schedule time to pause, observe, and reflect.** Much like becoming a more intuitive leader, having time on your calendar to pause, observe, and reflect is the mental and emotional exercise needed to continually assess your progress while creating space for crucial insights needed to direct or redirect your team's energy and focus.

Underlying these suggested interventions and approaches related to team development based on being a less directive, more intuitive, and more strategic leader is the need to create greater psychological safety for your team members. The most prestigious business and management publications and research outlets, including *Harvard Business Review* and *Massachusetts Institute of Technology (MIT) Sloan Management Review*, extol both the virtues and the productive outcomes of cultivating psychological safety in group settings. Essentially, psychological safety refers to the degree to which members of a team feel comfortable taking risks, expressing concerns, asking for help, and admitting mistakes without fear of reprisal or negative consequences. As previously discussed in Chapters 6 and 7, the common group decision-making dysfunctions found in both groupthink and the Abilene paradox are a result of a lack of group psychological safety and the ineffective communication patterns that emerge.

Now that we have adequately addressed the leadership growth opportunities required for becoming more self-actualized and less directive, let's turn our attention to the specific team cultures: detached, dramatic, and dependent. There are a number of unique strategies and interventions that teams can employ to help shift culture into a more dynamic state. Many of these recommended approaches are covered here, and additional team development activities and strategies are outlined in the Appendixes.

Developing Team Culture

Transforming the Detached Group Culture

The detached culture is the least effective level of team development, where members are disengaged and often disruptive based on underlying anger and apathy (i.e., fight/flight response) in the team's shadow (see Figure 10.2). It often leads to poor decision-making processes closely associated with groupthink. Leaders must focus on enhancing and improving the team shadow elements that include distraction, disengagement, and multiple, often competing, agendas that adversely impact a unified focus and inhibit any sense of the team all rowing in the same direction. Following are suggested practices and steps to help transform a detached culture:

» Provide candid feedback to the team's leader, letting them know the impact of the achiever style and fear of failure leadership shadow (e.g., micromanaging, being in the weeds, lack of delegation, etc.).
» Allow team members to acknowledge and vent any anger or frustration that exists below the surface, effectively managing any conflict between and among team members.
» Examine and resolve issues of authority and accountability to ensure that members are being fully utilized based on their experience and skillset (i.e., delegate more).

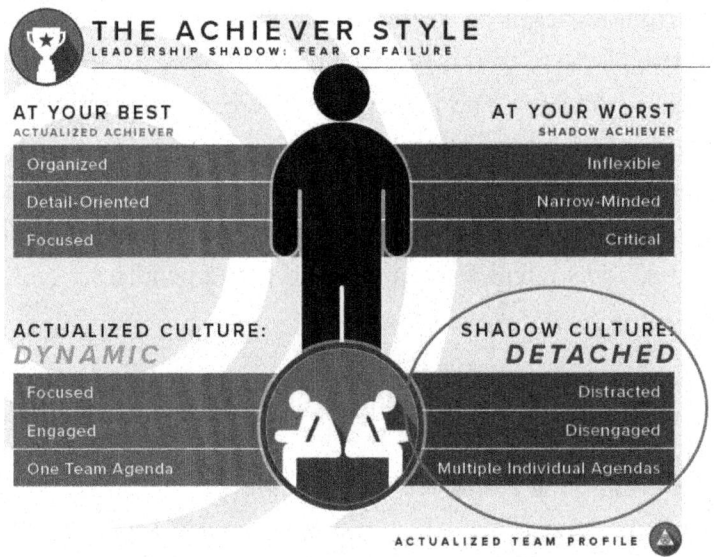

Figure 10.2. The achiever style: Detached

» Develop and implement broad decision-making processes that facilitate engagement, input, candor, and effective conflict management.

» Ensure that all members participate and adopt a "no cell phones" policy to ensure optimal engagement.

» Consider facilitating a team process to create a charter, values, or purpose statement that all members help create.

Transforming the Dramatic Group Culture

The dramatic culture represents a lower level of team development where members are personally committed to each other but often value relationships over results, which stems from underlying emotions of frustration and even despair in the team's shadow (see Figure 10.3). This culture is marked by excessive idealism, conflict avoidance, and unrealistic expectations for the future. The decision-making pitfall most common in this instance is the Abilene paradox and the inability to manage agreement. Leaders must focus on enhancing and improving the team shadow elements that include a lack of candor and honest communication, conflict

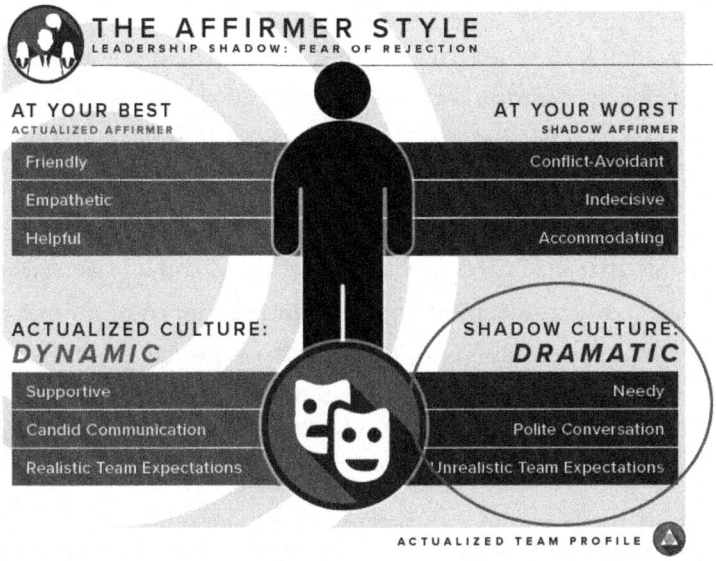

Figure 10.3. The affirmer style: Dramatic

avoidance, and excessive idealism that adversely impact productivity and performance. Following are suggested practices and steps to help transform the dramatic culture:

» Consider showing "The Abilene Paradox" video or providing the article to the team so that members better understand and can relate to the concept of mismanaged agreement.
» Encourage members to provide honest and candid feedback to both the leader and the other team members.
» Confront the team about poor performance, unrealistic expectations, or obvious problems (i.e., white elephants) that are adversely impacting productivity.
» Set challenging or even audacious performance goals for the team.
» Appoint individual members to serve as devil's advocate to critique the team's performance, plans, and decisions.
» Encourage members to express their true beliefs, feelings, doubts, and concerns to the team as a whole.

Transforming the Dependent Group Culture

The dependent culture represents the most common group culture, where members soften their true opinions in order to align with the leader or tradition, or may practice outright self-censorship (see Figure 10.4). This culture is marked by excessive reliance on the leader and tradition, and members are encouraged to get with the program. Leaders must focus on enhancing and improving the team shadow elements that include compliance, reactivity, and an overreliance on the leader which adversely impacts creativity, innovation, risk-taking, and shared accountability. Following are suggested strategies that can be implemented to transform the dependent culture:

» Provide clear goals and objectives for the team but allow individual members to develop their own unique approaches for execution.

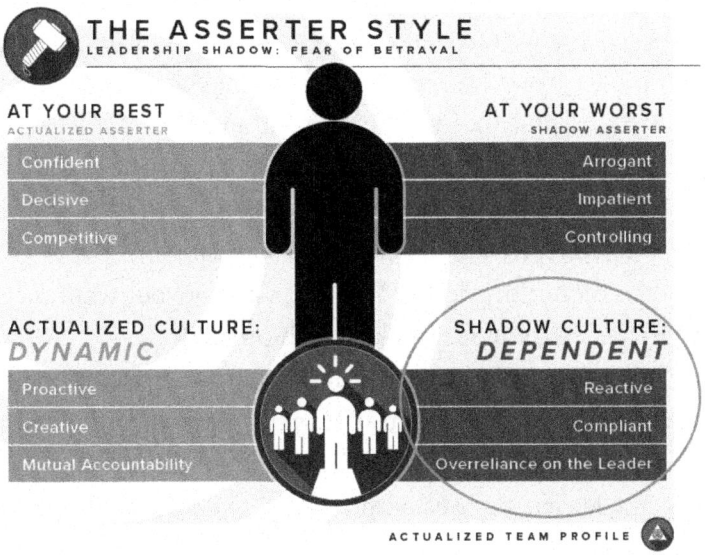

Figure 10.4. The asserter style: Dependent

» Create an environment where members feel safe disagreeing with the leader (and each other) and expressing their true opinions and beliefs.

» Allow members to clarify and communicate their roles and expectations to the entire team, including any frustrations they may be experiencing.

» Encourage the leader to delegate more.

» Provide the team members with as much information as possible to assist them in transitioning from dependence to interdependence.

» As a leader, recognize your role in creating and reinforcing the dependent cycle and commit to the team to be a partner in breaking this cycle and creating a more dynamic culture.

Maintaining the Dynamic Group Culture

The dynamic culture represents the highest level of group development and performance. Members are rational, responsible, and communicate directly and honestly with each other. There is a high level of engagement with the team and the overall organization, and members are committed to each other. The following strategies are suggested to maintain high levels of member engagement and to optimize performance in a dynamic culture:

» Protect the team from too many external distractions or influences (e.g., provide air cover for your team).
» Focus on healthy debate and discussion in your team meetings.
» Provide ongoing feedback to each other.
» Continue to define the long-term strategic goals and objectives, tweaking or radically adjusting as the environment dictates.
» Celebrate organizational successes and achievements.
» As the leader, stay out of the way!

The Team Transformation Cycle

Transformation at the individual level is challenging but achievable. When individuals are faced with difficult circumstances, such as their own mortality or a personal or professional setback, (e.g., divorce, job loss or demotion, etc.) they are often motivated to change themselves in a truly profound way. This shift or transformation results in seeing the world and themselves in a very different way. Individual transformation is also readily noticeable, and almost always welcome, by those closest to the individual.

In my last book, *Actualized Leadership*, I identified the three phases of personal transformation: vulnerability, responsibility, and forgiveness. In the first phase of vulnerability, we must be willing to put our guard down, suspend disbelief (especially if you are an asserter like me), and be open to feedback that often is disruptive. As the American philosopher Eric Hoffer (2006) stated, "In order to dispose a soul to action you must upset its equilibrium." Well, that adage doesn't just apply to individuals, it applies to teams as well.

In the second phase, responsibility, we must own our behavior and our mistakes, including our faulty assumptions about ourselves and others. It is crucial to take accountability for our part in our current state, and to commit to closing the gap between it and our future desired state.

Forgiveness, the final stage in individual transformation, combines personal accountability with letting go of wrongs and mistakes, both yours and what others have done to you, so that you can step into your highest potential. Special attention is given to the difference between forgiveness and condoning, emphasizing that not forgiving others ultimately holds us back. As the old saying goes, not forgiving others is like drinking poison and expecting the other party to suffer.

When thinking about shadow integration at the group level, and the team transformation process, there are four unique stages or phases that exist. Each phase affords a team an opportunity to get out of its collective comfort zone and both acknowledge and atone for any past mistakes while moving forward in concert as the leader, individual team members and the team as a whole actualize to their highest potential. The Team Transformation Cycle consists of four phases:

1. Assessment,
2. Acknowledgment,
3. Accountability, and
4. Assimilation.

Assessment is the first phase, and it is the foundation for all other processes and stages of team growth and development. This crucial first phase provides the X-ray or baseline for the current culture and state of performance, and it is from this objective assessment that the transformation process begins.

In the Actualized Teamwork Framework, I utilize the Actualized Team Profile which assesses the degree of culture and estimates the current level of team-actualization (i.e., the dynamic scale) for a working group. The value of this approach is that the profile results are based on the input of all the team members. The profile is not based on any one member's perspective or the analysis of the consultant or the leader. As such, it is much easier for the group to begin to see their culture for how it actually exists because it is more difficult to deflect or ignore.

Acknowledgment is the second phase in the Team Transformation Cycle, and this stage requires the leader and individual members to both accept the profile (i.e., culture results) and to acknowledge and own their individual behavior in helping to create, reinforce, and sustain the culture. Examples of acknowledgment may include an asserter leader who realizes that their behavior has led to the anxiety and fear underlying a culture of compliance and playing it safe instead of innovation and risk-taking. Or, individual members who may own that they passively agreed to an initiative that they never really supported or wanted to do and, as a result, have been withholding their energy and input while waiting for said initiative to fail. While these acts take courage and may be uncomfortable to discuss, they are essential if the group is to move forward and develop its full capacity and potential. As Jung often stated, the very act of an individual owning their shadow traits or projections is the first step on the path to individuation (i.e., self-actualization).

Accountability is the third phase of the transformation process and requires the energy and focus to shift from the past to the present and future. In this stage, the leader and individual members agree to new operating norms and processes and commit to being a part of a new team dynamic that will reward individuality, reasonable risk taking, candor, and the like. You can actually feel the energy in the room shift when you move into this third phase. Members often feel like a weight has been lifted because they've spoken their truth or confronted a situation that was upsetting and taking a lot of their psychic energy. Having effectively managed these team crucial conversations and acknowledged past mistakes, there is often a renewed sense of *us* and desire to move into a new future that supports both individual and team development.

The final phase in the Team Transformation Cycle, assimilation, is creating new group norms and expectations that will foster and facilitate a more dynamic way of working together. Members must stay alert to their need to communicate with candor (e.g., asking in meetings "Are we going to Abilene?," etc.) and commit to provide feedback with collegial candor to each other and to the leader. In this final phase, the rubber meets the road, and new operating agreements and working relationships are put to the test when both external organizational factors and internal team habits emerge under stress. It is crucial that the leader and the team stay the course and honor their new agreements to build trust and enhance the fragile state of psychological safety for the team.

Putting It All Together

If you're looking for a bottom line for this book, then I suppose this is it. My approach to team development uses a psychodynamic framework, which recognizes that teams, just like individuals, are impacted by their collective unconscious. My research has focused on both describing the unique team shadows, which are detached, dramatic, and dependent, and linking these cultures to specific leader styles (achiever, affirmer, and asserter.) Moreover, I have researched and validated interventions (see Appendixes) that help leaders and teams actualize their full collective potential.

While it is nearly impossible to boil it all down to one word, if I had to choose only one word it would be *communication*. If we have the courage of our convictions to communicate directly and honestly with each other in team settings, then we are better able to avoid the two classic pitfalls in team decision making: groupthink and the Abilene paradox. And while that sounds very easy, we've all been in team settings where our fear of being ostracized as a non-team player (or just fear of missing out in general) has held us back from speaking our truth.

The final section focused on team-actualization and dynamic culture, including an examination of the 5 dimensions of teamwork and the Team Transformation Cycle. Experiencing the process of both individual and team development and growth is the most satisfying part of my professional life. I think we often avoid this process because of the requirement to get outside of our comfort zone, sometimes way outside of our comfort zone, to effectively engage in team shadow acknowledgment. However, just like with individuals, I often implore people to do the work that is necessary to live a full, healthy life both professionally and personally. To loosely quote Abraham Maslow, every day we face the option to step into growth or retreat into fear. It is my sincere hope that will find the courage and compassion to actualize your and your team's potential and, in doing so, give others in your world permission to do the same.

PART V

APPENDIXES

Appendix A

Team Culture Style Summary

ACTUALIZED TEAM PROFILE REPORT

TEAM CULTURE STYLE SUMMARY

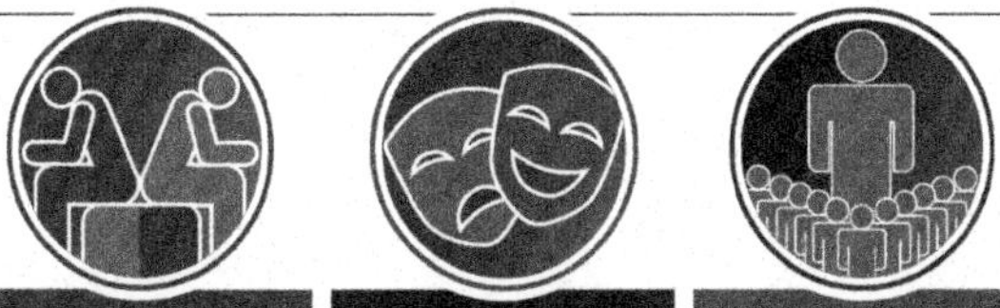

TEAM CULTURE	DETACHED	DRAMATIC	DEPENDENT
LEADER STYLE & SHADOW	ACHIEVER FEAR OF FAILURE	AFFIRMER FEAR OF REJECTION	ASSERTER FEAR OF BETRAYAL
ACTUALIZED CULTURE ATTRIBUTES	FOCUSED ENGAGED ONE TEAM AGENDA	SUPPORTIVE CANDID COMMUNICATION REALISTIC EXPECTATIONS	PROACTIVE CREATIVE MUTUAL ACCOUNTABILITY
SHADOW CULTURE ATTRIBUTES	DISTRACTED DISENGAGED MULTIPLE AGENDAS	NEEDY POLITE CONVERSATION UNREALISTIC EXPECTATIONS	REACTIVE COMPLIANT OVERRELIANCE ON LEADER
SHADOW EMOTIONS	ANGER AND APATHY	FRUSTRATION AND DESPAIR	FEAR AND ANXIETY
ACTUALIZING CULTURE INTERVENTIONS	CULTIVATE PARTICIPATION AND DELEGATION	CULTIVATE CANDOR AND FOCUS ON PERFORMANCE	CULTIVATE INDEPENDENCE AND SHARED ACCOUNTABILITY

Appendix B
The Culture Code Benchmark

ACTUALIZED TEAM PROFILE
CULTURE CODE BENCHMARK

DEPENDENT

DRAMATIC

MODERATE

MILD MILD

MILD

DETACHED

DYNAMIC	MILD	MODERATE	STRONG	INTENSE >/= 75
DETACHED	MILD </= 20	MODERATE	STRONG	INTENSE
DRAMATIC	MILD </= 30	MODERATE	STRONG	INTENSE
DEPENDENT	MILD	MODERATE </= 40	STRONG	INTENSE

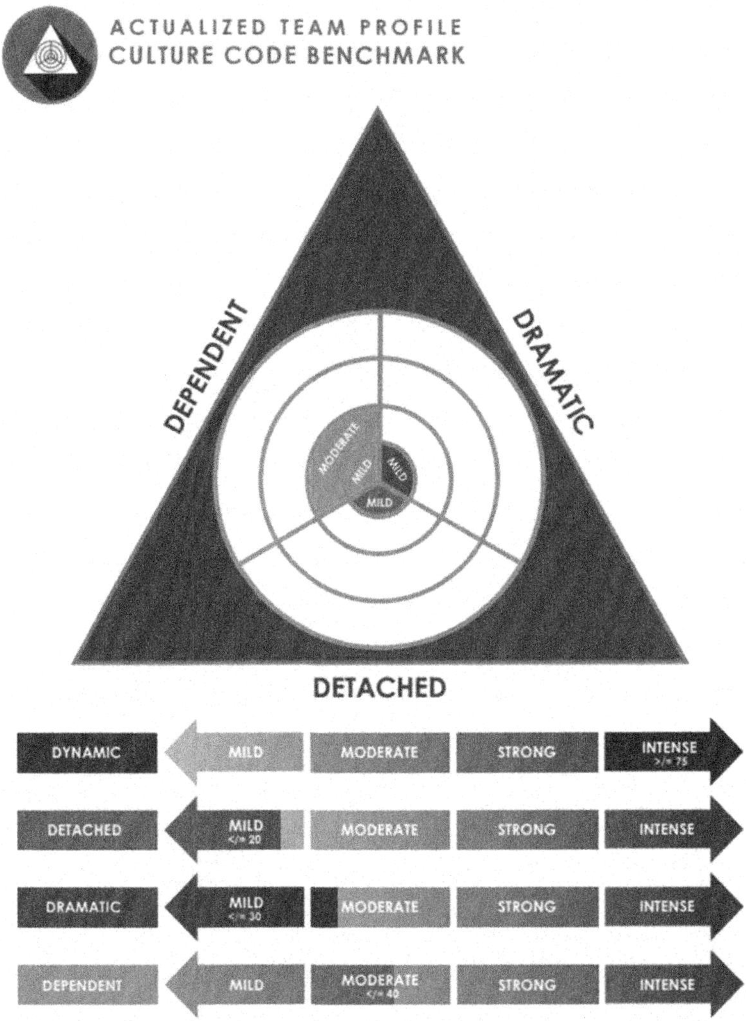

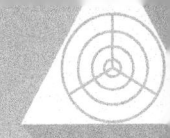

Appendix C

5 Dimensions Development Resource Guide

Dimension	Book	Article	Program/Video
Communication The degree to which your team communicates openly, candidly, and without hidden agendas during meetings.	*The Abilene Paradox* Jerry B. Harvey	"A Culture of Candor" James O'Toole & Warren Bennis	"The Power of Communication"
Conflict Management The degree to which conflict in your team is recognized and effectively managed in a productive manner.	*Crucial Conversations* Joseph Grenny, Jerry Patterson, Ron McMilian, Al Switzler & Emily Gregory	"How Management Teams Can Have a Good Fight" Kathleen M. Eisenhardt; Jean L. Kahwajy & L. J. Bourgeois	"3 Ways to Resolve a Conflict"
Engagement The degree to which each team member is engaged and actively participates in meetings and takes responsibility for achieving your team's goals.	*Thrive by Design: The Neuroscience that Drives High Performance Cultures* Don Rheem	"How Companies Can Improve Employee Engagement Right Now" Daniel Stein, Nick Hobson, Jon M. Jachimowicz & Ashley Whillians	"Are You an Ideal Team Player?"
Trust The degree to which team members trust each other and your leader, act in the best interest of the group, maintain confidentiality, and speak and act with transparency.	*Leaders Eat Last* Simon Sinek	"Managing a Polarized Workforce" Julia A. Minson & Francesca Gino	"8 Lessons on Building a Company People Enjoy Working For"
Purpose The degree to which your team has a sense of purpose and understanding of how your decisions and actions impact the larger goals and objectives of the organization.	*Find Your Way: A Practical Guide for Discovering Purpose for You and Your Team* Simon Sinek	"Creating a Purpose-Driven Organization" Robert E. Quinn & Anjan V. Thakor	"How Great Leaders Inspire Action"

Additional Harvard Business Review
Resources for Team Leaders

"The Leadership Odyssey," May–June 2023. Herminia Ibarra,
   Claudius A. Hildebrand, and Sabine Vinck

How to become a less directive leader and, in doing so, become
more strategic and create a more Actualized Team.

"How to Equip Your Team to Problem Solve Without You,"
   March 2023. Luis Velasquez and Kristin Gleitsman

How to break the cycle of micromanaging (umbrella management)
and allow your team to grow and flourish to their full potential.

"Fixing a Self-Sabotaging Team," March–April 2023. N. Anand
   and Jean-Louis Barsoux

How to apply a psychodynamic approach, specifically through the
lens of Wilfred Bion, for identifying and managing underlying problems adversely impacting team performance and member satisfaction. The actualized team profile (ATP) is built on Bion's model for
group culture.

Appendix D
Team Purpose Worksheet

ACTUALIZED TEAMWORK

OUR PURPOSE WORKSHEET

OUR TEAM PURPOSE

MY LEADERSHIP PURPOSE

OUR SHADOW TEAM *(OFF-PURPOSE)*

What others will see in our behavior.

How others will feel when working with us.

The implication for the organization.

OUR ACTUALIZED TEAM *(ON-PURPOSE)*

What others will see in our behavior.

How others will feel when working with us.

The implication for the organization.

Appendix E
Team Intervention Handbook

Tools to Open Team Meetings

Centering

Centering is a process that allows team members to quiet their minds and collectively exhale together. Allowing members to center before starting a meeting creates a sense of inner balance and peace, and it facilitates a greater sense of focus and engagement. Centering may be extremely open-ended or focused, such as concentrating on a word, phrase, or object. For example, team members can be asked to close their eyes, go inside themselves, and focus on their breathing, allowing all parts of themselves to achieve greater balance. You can center for three, five, or ten minutes, either in silence or with spa music or nature sounds playing the background. Here are some suggestions for starting a centering session before a team meeting:

1. Explain that you are going to take a few minutes before officially starting the meeting to allow participants to center themselves.
2. Ask team members to sit up straight in their chairs with their feet flat on the floor.
3. If they are comfortable doing so, ask them to close their eyes.
4. Finally, ask participants to focus on their breathing and to pay attention to what comes into their mind without judgment.

Check-In

A useful approach after centering is to allow all members of the team to check in. The approach should be completely voluntary and informal, asking participants that would like to check in to let the team know what's on their mind, what challenges (personally and professionally) may have come up during the centering, and what they may need from the team during the meeting. Allow everyone an opportunity to check in before starting the formal part of the meeting.

Visualization and Guided Imagery

There are times when using visualization and a guided imagery process helps team members easily identify solutions to performance barriers that are often internally imposed. Many successful individuals, including Tiger Woods, Oprah Winfrey, Phil Jackson, and Michael Jordan, extol the virtues of visualization and guided imagery on helping to create optimal performance. The process often externalizes answers and solutions based on the way in which a person represents objects and experiences in their mind. Visualization can be either receptive, allowing images and impressions to surface, or active, consciously creating what is desired to be felt or experienced. Receptive visualization works by reducing the analytical activity of the brain (left brain), allowing unconscious thoughts, emotions, and intuitive insights to emerge (right brain). An example of this is when the answer to a problem emerges in a state of quiet reflection. In guided imagery, a facilitator suggests the outline of an experience and the person engages in the process with their own personal preferences, ideas, and intuition. Just like with visualization, guided imagery works by allowing the person to release the analytical part of their mind to a guide who leads them to receive information from the intuitive part of the mind. There are numerous visualization and guided imagery resources available in books and online.

Tools to Define Team Challenges

Brainstorming

Purpose

Brainstorming is used to generate a large number of ideas or solutions in a short period of time. Brainstorming encourages creativity and produces many alternatives, thus increasing the probability of uncovering the optimal choice, answer, or solution. It is a fun, easy, and enjoyable way to open a session or meeting.

Materials Needed
» Flipchart
» Markers
» Masking tape

Ground Rules for Brainstorming
» *Rule 1: Avoid evaluation or criticism of ideas.*
   Premature evaluation or criticism of ideas will reduce the effectiveness of idea generation. This rule is critical and should be strictly enforced.
» *Rule 2: Encourage a large quantity of suggestions.*
   The more ideas, the better the chances are of finding the best idea.
» *Rule 3: Encourage out-of-the-box thinking.*
   Out-of-the-box thinking means encouraging participants to be uninhibited and to come up with wild, outrageous ideas which might actually end up being among the most desirable ideas.

Process

Brainstorming involves three steps:

1. Generate ideas,
2. Clarify ideas, and
3. Combine similar ideas.

Generate Ideas

» Introduce the session and draw the participants' attention to the issue statement.

» Have the recorder write all responses on flipchart pages and hang the full pages on the wall where participants can read them. Make sure responses are recorded as closely as possible to the participants' own wording.

» As you approach the time limit, give a five-minute warning. This will allow everyone to contribute one last idea.

» Stop the idea generation at the designated time unless it stops naturally.

Clarify Ideas

» Read each idea to the group, and ask what questions there are about the ideas.

» As questions arise, have the points clarified by the person who gave the response, and continue through the list until you reach the end.

» Avoid debating the importance or worthiness of an idea.

Combine Similar Ideas

» Combine the ideas that are nearly identical if appropriate. This is not the same as categorization of the ideas.

For example:

> "Leadership development" and "training and development" may be combined into one idea.

» Look for easy agreements on similar ideas. Do not let the group get too caught up in arguing over the similarity of ideas. Reach consensus in three steps:

> Present the idea: "Linda suggests we combine leadership development with training and development."

> Check for understanding: "Is this clear to everyone?"

> Check for agreement: "Is there anyone who cannot agree with this?"

» Ideas cannot be combined if disagreement exists. Try to combine only two ideas at a time.

Best Practices
» Ensure that participation among group members is equal. Use a round-robin format as one way to deal with dominators or withdrawers. Go around the room, and let each participant present an idea. Continue this process until all ideas are recorded or until time is out.
» Set a goal at the beginning of the session to generate a certain number of ideas. This can speed up the process and increase participant motivation.
For example:
> "Let's try to get twenty items in the next ten minutes."
» Be aware that superficial ideas can result from the freewheeling atmosphere. Be careful not to limit creativity when responding to such ideas. An outrageous idea may lead to a workable solution.
» Ask "what if" during a brainstorming session when the group seems to run out of ideas. Asking unconventional questions can help to vary the group's perspective on an issue and may lead to more ideas:
For example:
> What if we became a training vendor and sold our programs to other organizations?
> What if we outsourced some of our work?
> What if we bought our competitors' operations and offices?

These techniques allow participants to write ideas rather than state them aloud, which encourages equal participation among group members. Use the techniques if you feel there are ineffective dominators or influencers in the group.

Imaging

Purpose

Use imaging to allow group members to creatively visualize their idea of the issue. Participants can work in groups or as individuals. This process allows a group to address an issue from a non-traditional, nonverbal perspective. It also encourages *breakthrough thinking*—which means going beyond traditional boundaries to produce creative solutions to problems.

Materials

» Flipchart
» Markers
» Tape

Process

1. Ask group members to draw colorful images of the issue on a flipchart page.
   For example:
   › Draw your ideal job.
   › Draw the causes of the problem.
   › Draw the solution of the problem.
2. Tell group members not to use words in the drawing itself.
3. When drawings are complete, allow individuals or groups to explain their drawings to the larger group.
4. A number of follow-up techniques can be used at this point.
   For example:
   › Have individuals develop a personal vision or mission statement based on the images drawn.

Is/Is Not

Purpose

Use the Is/Is Not technique to define components of an issue. This technique is useful if the group is having trouble defining or agreeing on the issue or problem.

Materials
» Flipchart
» Markers
» Masking tape

Process
1. Divide a flipchart page into two columns labeled "Is" and "Is Not."
2. Ask participants to describe the issue.
3. Write the facts about the issue in the "Is" column.
4. Write what is not part of the issue in the "Is Not" column.
5. A variety of options exist at this point to continue analyzing the problem or begin recommending strategies to resolve the issue. *For example:*
   › Write a clear issue statement, and brainstorm ideas for dealing with the issue.
   › Use the "Is" and the "Is Not" information to keep the group focused on the real issues.

Tools to Solve Team Challenges

Nominal Group Technique
Purpose
Nominal Group Technique (NGT) is a structured process specifically designed to generate ideas and produce group consensus. It works particularly well in small groups of five to twelve individuals. With more than twelve participants, divide into two or more groups. NGT can be used in situations requiring problem identification or in solution-oriented meetings when it is desirable to:

» Obtain ideas from all group members in a short period of time.
» Evoke maximum participation from each person.

» Focus the group's concentration on a specific question.
» Reach a group consensus through voting.
» Have a clear picture of the next steps at the end of the meeting.

Materials

» Flipchart
» Markers
» Tape
» Paper
» Pens/Pencils
» 3" × 5" index cards
» Post-It Notes (optional)

Process

The NGT process involves five steps:

1. Silent idea generation,
2. Report ideas,
3. Clarify, combine, and categorize ideas,
4. Rank importance of ideas, and
5. Vote.

Silent Idea Generation

» Be sure group members have a clear understanding of the issue and the background knowledge to address it.
» Write an open-ended issue statement on a flipchart page. Read the issue statement aloud.
» Tell participants to write their ideas and solutions on a sheet of paper in succinct verb/noun statements.
   For example:
   › "Increase sales."
» Tell the participants to work individually and silently.
» Allow five to ten minutes for this stage.

Report Ideas

» Use a round-robin method to go around the table and ask each member to say one of their ideas in a brief sentence without any explanation or justification.

» Ask the recorder to write each response on the flipchart as rapidly as possible in the participant's own words. Avoid abbreviating or interpreting ideas.

» Label each response with a letter of the alphabet.

» Post filled flipchart pages on the wall so the group can see them.

» Continue going around the room until every participant has exhausted their list of ideas.

Clarify, Combine, and Categorize Ideas

» Read each idea on the flipchart pages aloud in sequence, and ask for comments.

For example:

› "What questions or comments do you have regarding Item A?" As questions arise, discuss the idea to clarify meaning and logic. It is important to avoid debating the importance or worthiness of an item.

» Combine nearly identical ideas (if appropriate). This is not the same as categorizing ideas.

» Ask the group to read the list of ideas and decide which ideas fit in categories. Again, group consensus is required to categorize any ideas.

Rank Importance of Ideas

» Distribute 3" × 5" index cards to each participant.

» Ask each participant to select and record one idea per card for the five items or categories they consider the best or highest priority from the list.

» Ask participants to spread the five cards out and decide which item is most important, followed by the second most important, etc. Participants should *write the number 5* on the card with the *most* important idea, the *number 4* on the *second* most important, and so on.

» As you collect the cards, check each one for completeness.
» Tally the votes on the flipchart in a different colored marker.
» Summarize the final vote on a separate flipchart page.
» Consider using the following *shortcut voting process*:
   › Distribute five Post-It notes to each participant.
   › Ask participants to number the notes from one to five. Each participant votes by placing the number 5 note on the flipchart next to the idea they consider *most* important, the number 4 note on the *second* most important idea, and so on.
   › Individuals cannot stack their votes by placing more than one note on an idea.
   › Add the numbers on the notes next to each idea. Write the total next to the idea. Remove the notes from the flipchart.

   Note: It is important that the number 5 note be placed on the most important idea and the number 1 note be placed on the fifth most important idea. When tallied, the more important ideas are indicated by higher scores.

Vote

» Examine the voting pattern for inconsistencies or discrepancies (e.g., one person gave a particular item a "5" but no one else gave it *any* votes).
» Discuss each of the items again briefly to further clarify.
» Hold the final vote.

Force Field Analysis

Purpose

The Force Field Analysis technique provides a framework for problem solving and implementing planned change. The process involves determining those forces that will drive the change and those forces that will block the change. It is effective for defining and analyzing problems as well as developing action plans.

The two forces are as follows:

- **Driving forces**: Factors or pressures that strongly support the goals of change.
  For example:
  - Changing technology,
  - Client demand for an innovative product, or
  - Changing work force.
- **Restraining forces**: Factors that act as obstacles to change.
  For example:
  - Lack of necessary skills,
  - Employee resistance, or
  - Insufficient resources to support change.

Change can be significantly facilitated through the strengthening of driving forces and or the weakening or eliminating of restraining forces (see Figure E.1).

FORCE FIELD ANALYSIS

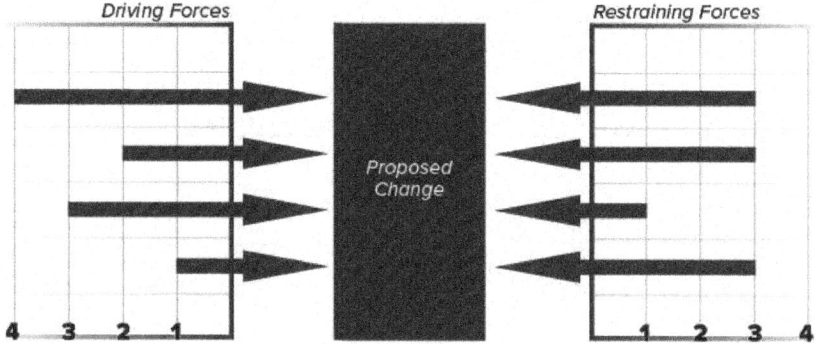

Figure E.1. Force Field Analysis

Materials
» Flipchart
» Markers
» Tape
» Post-It Notes

Process
Force Field Analysis involves five steps:

1. Identify issue,
2. Identify forces,
3. Identify critical forces, and
4. Develop action plan.

Identify Issue
» Tell team members to envision and list components of the ideal situation.
» Ask participants to share their ideas. Write the components on a flipchart.
» Tell group members to list components of the present situation.
» Again, ask participants to share their ideas. Write the components on a flipchart.
   Note: In some circumstances, the issue may be identified and the first step can be omitted.
   For example:
   › A departmental reorganization is planned.
   › A new mission or vision statement is drafted.
   › Aspects of the present situation are desirable, and the influence of change should be avoided.
» In these cases, begin with Step 2 and identify forces.

Identify Forces
» Brainstorm a list of ideas that act as driving forces to encourage the change from the present situation to the ideal situation.

» Brainstorm a list of restraining forces that inhibit the change from the present situation to the ideal situation.

Identify Critical Forces

» Write the top ideas on a new flipchart page. This reduces the distraction at the entire original list.

» Give each group member a Post-It Note for each item on the narrowed list.

» Tell each participant to evaluate each item based on a five-point Likert scale.

For example:

› "Evaluate each item on a scale of zero to five, with five being 'a very influential force' and zero being 'no force.' Write the number on a Post-It Note and place it next to the item on the flipchart."

» Tally the values assigned to each item. Then tally the values assigned to all the items in the restraining forces column and then all the items in the driving forces column. Compare the influential power of the two columns. For example, if the restraining forces total thirty points and the driving forces only fifteen points, then the restraining forces are more influential on the change.

Develop Action Steps

» Develop a specific strategy for changing each of the strongest forces to move from the present situation to the desired situation. Strategies may involve one of the following:

› Reduce or weaken the resisting forces.

› Increase or strengthen the driving forces.

› Create additional driving forces.

› Combination of the above.

» Use the action plan chart to define *who*, will do *what*, by *when*, with *what resources*, and *how* performance will be measured.

Fishbone (Cause-and-Effect) Diagram

Purpose

Use the Fishbone Diagram, also known as the Cause-and-Effect Diagram, to explore cause-and-effect relationships (see Figure E.2). This technique visually displays the causes of a condition or issue. Performance measures can be developed from the results.

Materials

» Flipchart
» Markers
» Masking tape

Process

1. Write the effect or outcome on the right side of the diagram.
   For example:
   › The payroll is over budget for the development stage of the project.

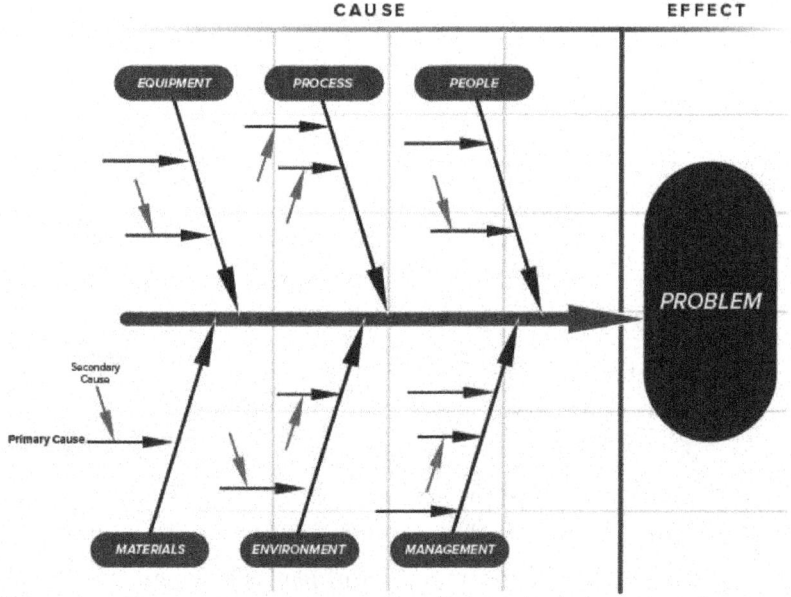

Figure E.2. The Fishbone Diagram

2. Write the four major categories on the left side of the diagram. The categories can be equipment, policies and procedures, information, people, perceptions, environment, or any others that are appropriate for the topic.

3. Brainstorm a list of potential causes, and write them on the lines of the diagram.

Appendix F

Dynamic Team Decision Making: Managing Conflict and Agreement

Managing Team Conflict: Groupthink*

Steps to Break the Groupthink Decision-Making Cycle:

1. What is our current team culture? Does our culture lend itself to groupthink?
2. How directive is our leader?
3. Do you feel pressure to "get on board" or "be a team player?"
4. Are you comfortable communicating a different perspective or viewpoint to the team?

How many of the following symptoms exist in your team?

» An illusion of invulnerability.
» Collective efforts to rationalize or minimize warnings.
» Unquestioned belief in the group's inherent morality.
» Stereotyped views of outsiders as enemies.
» Direct pressure exerted on members to conform.
» Self-censorship of individual beliefs and feelings.
» Shared illusion of unanimity.

Prescriptions for Managing Team Conflict:

- » Assign members the role of critical evaluator or devil's advocate.
- » Ask outside subject matter experts for their input and opinions.
- » Consider the potential consequences of a poor decision.
- » Break the team into subgroups to address process issues.
- » Create a psychologically safe environment where team members are encouraged to communicate directly with candor.

Note: Video training by Media Partners provides a comprehensive team development solution for dealing with groupthink I personally recommend.

Managing Team Agreement: The Abilene Paradox*

Steps to Break the Abilene Paradox Decision-Making Cycle:

1. What is our current team culture? Does our culture lend itself to the Abilene paradox?
2. How directive is our leader?
3. Do you feel internal pressure to agree with the team's recommendation?
4. Are you comfortable communicating a different perspective or viewpoint to the team?

How many of the following symptoms exist in your team?

- » Individuals privately acknowledge their true opinions and beliefs about both the problem(s) and solution(s), but fail to communicate them in a team setting.
- » While members are cordial and agreeable, frustration with the decision-making process exists below the surface.
- » It seems that the desire to be accepted by the group outweighs any desire to express concerns or challenge assumptions.
- » Team decisions are based on the perceived agreement of the members.

Prescriptions for Managing Team Agreement:

» Consider what is potentially at stake and have the courage of your convictions to speak out and convey your true beliefs and feelings.

» Consider the potential consequences of a poor decision.

» Break the team into subgroups to address process issues.

» Create a psychologically safe environment where team members are encouraged to communicate directly with candor.

*Note: Video training by Media Partners provides a comprehensive team development solution for dealing with the Abilene paradox I personally recommend.

Appendix G
What's Your Team Culture? A Role-Play Simulation

What's Your Team Culture?: A Role-Play Simulation (WTC) is a structured simulation that allows participants to explore the concept of group culture and team dynamics from a psychodynamic perspective. The purpose of this experiential learning exercise is to introduce the unique levels of team culture and group dynamics using a psychodynamic framework in order to assist participants in developing the necessary skills for identifying and regulating the emotions associated with small group behavior. This highly interactive session allows participants to discuss the concepts related to teamwork and group dynamics and develop strategies for improving team performance.

Overview
The facilitator provides an introduction and overview of the relevant framework and concepts for this simulation. After an introduction to the basic concepts of WTC, group culture, and team dynamics, participants read a statement that is associated with one of the four levels of group culture which follow: detached, dramatic, dependent, and dynamic. The participants engage in a group learning exercise and role-play simulation to demonstrate the impact of the underlying emotionality on team culture and performance. The specific skills necessary for ascertaining the level of group culture, as well as strategies for improving a group's performance, are discussed.

Goals of the Simulation

» Introduce the concepts of the impact of underlying emotionality on team culture in order to better understand the impact that emotions have on group performance and member satisfaction.

» Describe the four distinct levels of team culture and the leadership styles associated with each culture: detached (achiever), dramatic (affirmer), dependent (asserter), and dynamic (actualized).

» Teach participants the requisite skills necessary for correctly identifying group emotionality, and the corresponding level of culture, based on the behaviors and communication patterns of group members.

» Facilitate discussion among the participants about unique experiences in groups, both positive and negative, and how these experiences provide insights into the concept of underlying emotionality on team culture and performance.

Group Size

This simulation is intended for groups ranging in total size from twelve to forty, with subgroups ranging in size from three to ten in order to complete the simulation.

Time Required

Approximately ninety minutes are required for the simulation (thirty minutes for the introduction, thirty minutes for the simulation, and thirty minutes for discussion).

Intended Audience

Existing small groups and teams in organizational settings.

Physical Setting

A large room with movable chairs is needed for the simulated team meetings to occur where participants can observe the role plays.

Playing the Game

» The facilitator begins the simulation by discussing the concepts central to the goal of this role-play: the underlying emotionality of group culture, leadership styles, and the resulting team dynamics that ensue. This overview includes introducing the concepts of the detached, the dramatic, the dependent, and the dynamic modes of group behavior, as well as the leadership styles associated with each culture (achiever > detached, affirmer > dramatic, asserter > dependent, and actualized > dynamic).

» After the overview, participants choose one of the WTC Identifying Statements, and read the statement out loud. *Note:* The facilitator will need to copy, cut, and fold the statements so that they are randomly chosen out of a hat or some other vessel.

» Participants read their statement aloud to entire group. The entire group as a whole decides which level of team culture is illustrated with each statement, and the participants organize together around each distinct level culture (i.e., detached, dramatic, dependent, and dynamic). *Note:* The facilitator should be sure that the group's consensus for each WTC Identifier Statement is correct with the actual level of group culture it is meant to illustrate.

» Once the group as a whole agrees which culture the statement belongs to, the participant who read the WTC Identifier Statement joins that group. *Note:* You may want to have the four corners of the room labeled with each group culture name.

» After everyone has read their statement and the four groups have been formed, the facilitator distributes *The Acme Industries Situational Appraisal* to the participants. The groups break out into private sessions for fifteen minutes to review the situation and to develop their role-play based on the situational appraisal. Their role-play will be presented to the entire group. Each of the WTC Identifier Statements should be woven into their role-play. One participant from each group should assume the role of the team leader, adopt the appropriate leadership style (e.g., achiever, etc.), and role play that style's approach to managing others, focusing especially on the leadership shadow traits of that particular style. For example, if the group is detached and the leader is an achiever, then they may want to engage in obsessive criticism and micromanaging behaviors to illustrate the impact of leader style and shadow on team culture.

» The small groups reconvene and present their role-plays to the entire group to illustrate the five distinct levels of team culture. The role-plays should be presented in the following order: detached, dramatic, dependent, and dynamic.

» Participants are encouraged to discuss the feedback presented by the process observers and facilitator. This discussion should allow members to express their thoughts during the role play and to provide examples of similar experiences of group cultures in organizational settings.

Discussion

Appreciating the impact of emotionality in group behavior is not a new concept or endeavor. French sociologists from the 1800s Gustav Lebon and Emile Durkheim, as well as psychoanalysts from the 1900s Sigmund Freud and Carl Jung, were some of the forerunners of attempts to better understand small group behavior from both a sociological and a psychological perspective. The WTC Simulation is based on a psychological perspective, specifically a psychodynamic approach for understanding group dynamics in team settings.

The Psychodynamic Perspective of Team Culture

There are numerous frameworks or lenses to view small group behavior and team dynamics. From my perspective, the psychodynamic lens is not only the most valid, it also possesses the greatest utility in creating lasting, positive change in organizations. The psychodynamic perspective focuses on the impact that the unconscious has on human behavior. In the broadest sense, the psychodynamic approach for understanding group behavior can be classified into two categories: psychoanalytic and humanistic (McLeod and Kettner-Polley, 2004). The psychoanalytic approach falls under the *medical* metaphor, with an emphasis on diagnosis and description. In this camp, the works of Sigmund Freud, Wilfred Bion, and Carl Jung are paramount. The humanistic approach falls under the *developmental* metaphor, with an emphasis on learning and prescription. In this camp, the works of Kurt Lewin, Abraham Maslow, and again Carl Jung, are the most influential.

Wilfred Bion is arguably the most influential thinker, researcher, and writer in small group behavior and the concept of team culture. Not only did Bion agree with Freud and Jung that the unconscious was a crucial part of group life, he was able to classify and categorize the collective shadow found in groups. Wilfred Bion's seminal work in group behavior is predicated on the unconscious and underlying emotionality of the groups. Bion (1961) postulated that when groups of three or more come together, a collective mental activity takes place. This process allows the group to express underlying assumptions and form common perceptions. As a result of this activity, two distinct types of group behavior occur simultaneously: a work group and a basic assumption group. The work group is the overt, rational side of the group focused on the explicit task. The work group is grounded in reality. When it is the predominant mode of group behavior, the group members are able to contain their anxieties and effectively engage in creative problem-solving and learning. The basic assumption group is the covert, irrational side of the group and is composed of the unconscious fears and anxieties of the group members. The basic assumption group is irrational, grounded in fantasy, and prevents the group from engaging in effective problem-solving and learning.

Basic assumptions emerging in group cultures operate in an "as-if" mode, such that the group acts as if an external force exists that threatens the group's well-being. There are four types of basic assumption mental states: dependency, fight, flight, and pairing. In the fight/flight mode, the group members act as if there is an external force threatening their existence from which they must flee. This is the most primitive stage of group development emerging from the primal survival fight/flight mechanism which is amplified in group settings. This basic assumption group is impulsive and non-reflective and is characterized by apathy, withdrawal, and frustration. The flight level of team culture is classified as detached.

The pairing group acts as if a new leader or product will provide salvation for the group's existence. Harmony and hopeful expectation mark this basic assumption group, where excessive idealism and unrealistic aspirations abound. This level of team culture is referred to as dramatic.

In the dependency mode, group members act as if the purpose of the meeting is to allow an all-knowing leader to protect and lead them. Group members follow the charismatic leader without question and take no responsibility for their actions or decisions. The dependency level of team culture is classified as dependent.

The work group classified as the dynamic culture is the most mature level of group development and the highest level of team culture. Open communication, creative problem solving, and synergistic learning mark this stage of group development. Members are accountable to each other, diverse views are sought, and team members have a resilient optimism for the future. Table 2.1 provides a summary of the psychodynamic foundations of actualized teamwork.

As previously discussed, the four approaches to leader style in the actualized leadership profile (ALP) Framework can be plotted on two dimensions: orientation and problem-solving. Orientation refers to mindset and focus of the leader. There are two distinct approaches that emerge: tactical and strategic. A more tactical orientation is a short-term, execution-focused approach that may be best described as rational, pragmatic, tangible, planned, practical, and cautious. The achiever and affirmer styles are more tactical. A more strategic orientation is a long-term, results-focused approach that may be best described as big-picture, holistic, imaginative, spontaneous, objective, and risky. The asserter and actualized styles are more strategic.

The second dimension is based on problem solving and decision-making. There are two basic approaches that emerge: logical and intuitive. A more logical approach to problem-solving favors rationality, data, predictability, sensibility, process, and procedure. The achiever and asserter styles are more logical. A more intuitive approach to problem solving favors inference, novelty, gut-feel, sixth sense, imagination, and play. The affirmer and actualized styles are more intuitive. Figure 2.2 provides a summary overview of the four approaches to leadership plotted on the two dimensions of orientation and problem-solving, yielding a 2×2 matrix.

Similar to the leadership styles, another 2×2 matrix for team culture can be created (see Figure 2.3). But, more importantly, it can also be mapped onto Figure 2.3 as an extension of leader style. As such, you can visually see what I refer to as the actualized performance cube (APC), which illustrates the connection between leader style and culture. The team culture matrix is based on two dimensions: performance and results and people and relationships. Performance and results refers to the overall effectiveness of the team in accomplishing goals and productivity, classified as either low or high.

The second dimension is people and relationships, and this refers to the overall engagement and connection that team members experience intrinsically, also classified as either low or high. The detached and dependent cultures are cooler and tend to have members that are less engaged and satisfied. The dramatic and dynamic cultures are warmer and tend to have members that are more engaged and satisfied.

Figure 2.4 combines both the leader and team matrices to create the actualized performance cube (APC).

The Acme Merger Situational Appraisal

Based on the scenario below, your group should develop a five-to seven-minute role-play that demonstrates the emotions, attitudes, and behaviors of the level of team culture represented by your group culture assignment. Feel free to be as creative as possible in showcasing your level of culture. You may want to include both verbal and nonverbal examples to illustrate your team's culture. Each participant should incorporate their statement into the role-play.

Your company, Acme Industries, is an international leader in widget production and sales. The downturn in the economy, coupled with increased competition, has lowered sales and decreased revenue. Last year, Acme underwent a major restructuring initiative with a 15 percent reduction in force. Unfortunately, company performance failed to improve. In an effort to save the company, Acme has just announced that it will merge with your prime competitor, Widgets-R-Us, Inc.

You have been selected to be a member of the transition team for the merger. As a change agent, you and your team members are charged with trying to make the transition as smooth as possible. Information concerning the merger has been very sketchy. As you take your seat for the team's first meeting, you wonder what the future will hold. . .

WTC Identifier Statement

Detached Team Culture
1. Criticism and blame abound in our team meetings.
2. We often seem detached.
3. Some of us are guilty of leaving meetings early.
4. We often act as if we would prefer to be somewhere else.
5. Some of us routinely arrive late to meetings.
6. We tend to drift off task.
7. We often fail to participate.

8. We often engage in open conflict.

9. We are hostile towards each other.

10. We often interrupt each other.

Dramatic Team Culture

1. Members are careful not to hurt anyone's feelings.

2. We often ignore obvious problems.

3. We hope for the best.

4. We are unrealistically optimistic about our future.

5. Members want to be accepted by the group at any cost.

6. We are more concerned about maintaining harmony than in getting work done.

7. We enjoy a warm, supportive atmosphere.

8. We are highly supportive of each other.

9. We have a very warm and friendly atmosphere.

10. We ignore obvious problems.

Dependent Team Culture

1. We often ask for guidance.

2. We rely heavily on rules and procedures.

3. Some of us act immaturely.

4. We are unable to manage our time effectively.

5. Our leader knows what's best for us.

6. We often wait to be told what to do.

7. We often appeal to our leader for direction.

8. We avoid making decisions and taking accountability.

9. We keep our head down and play it safe.

10. We never challenge our boss.

Dynamic Team Culture

1. We appreciate different opinions.

2. We manage our time effectively.

3. New ideas are expressed freely.

4. We provide thoughtful feedback to each other.

5. We communicate directly and honestly with each other.
6. We are effective listeners.
7. We stay focused on, and committed to, the task.
8. We set realistic goals and work towards them.
9. We are resilient and optimistic about our future.
10. We seek relevant information, often from outside our group.

Appendix H

Technical Statement: Reliability and Validity for the ATP

The purpose of Appendix H is to demonstrate the validity and reliability for the *Actualized Team Profile* (ATP) survey, both the long-form and the short-form versions.[*] Additionally, findings are presented that establish the link between leader style (as measured by the *Actualized Leader Profile* [ALP]) and the four levels of team culture.

The ATP is a twenty-five-item self-report assessment that measures team culture based on the underlying emotionality of group members in a four-component solution using a framework established by Wilfred Bion. Bion's (1961) research and framework provides a valid and reliable model for understanding the impact of unconscious or underlying emotionality on performance and members satisfaction in group and team settings. Bion was the first to classify four modes of group culture based on the *basic assumption mental states* (BAMS) of group members, which represent their collective unconscious emotionality. The ATP framework has been enhanced by the works of Carl Jung, Herbert Thelen, Dorothy Stock, and Jerry B. Harvey.

Validity for the ATP was established using a Principal Components Factor Analysis (PCFA) to ascertain both the number of factors (four) and the factor loadings for each survey item on the four scales.

---

[*] The ATP short-form (free ATP) is a subset of the larger *Actualized Leader Profile* (ALP) long-form assessment. The word-pair section of this technical report provides the statistical information and reliability for these items that connect leader style to team culture.

A four-factor model with eigenvalues greater than 1.0 was generated, and survey items were reduced from forty to twenty based on the factor loading scores. The statistical PCFA analyses support a four-factor model of team culture and group behavior. The four-factor model in the PCFA analysis includes detached (fight/flight), dramatic (pairing), dependent (dependency), and dynamic (work).

The additional five items assess the degree to which members perceive the *5 dimensions of teamwork*. Eigenvalues ranged from 14.13–1.99 and accounted for 42 percent of the observed variance. The reliability for the ATP was estimated by assessing the internal consistency of the survey items for each of the four scales (i.e., detached, dramatic, dependent, and dynamic) by calculating Cronbach's alpha for each scale item. The standardized item Cronbach's alpha for the four scales ranged from 0.706 to 0.881. The research effort is summarized, and conclusions are drawn with specific implications for leadership development.

Introduction

Bion (1961) postulated that when groups of three or more come together, a collective mental activity takes place. This process allows the group to express underlying assumptions and form common perceptions. As a result of this activity, two distinct types of group behavior occur simultaneously: a work group and a basic assumption group. The work group is the overt, rational side of the group focused on the explicit task. The work group is grounded in reality. When it is the predominant mode of group behavior, the group members are able to contain their anxieties and effectively engage in creative problem solving and learning. The basic assumption group is the covert, irrational side of the group and is composed of the unconscious fears and anxieties of the group members. The basic assumption group is irrational, grounded in fantasy, and prevents the group from engaging in effective problem-solving and learning.

Basic assumptions emerging in group cultures operate in an "as-if" mode, such that the group acts as if an external force exists that threatens the group's well-being. There are four types of basic assumption mental states: dependency, fight, flight, and pairing. In the fight/flight mode, the group members act as if there is an external force threatening their existence from which they must flee. This is the most primitive stage of group development emerging from the primal survival fight/flight mechanism which is amplified in group settings. This basic assumption group is impulsive and non-reflective and is characterized by apathy, withdrawal, and frustration. The flight level of team culture is classified as detached.

The pairing group acts as if a new leader or product will provide salvation for the group's existence. Harmony and hopeful expectation mark this basic assumption group, where excessive idealism and unrealistic aspirations abound. This level of team culture is referred to as dramatic.

In the dependency mode, group members act as if the purpose of the meeting is to allow an all-knowing leader to protect and lead them. Group members follow the charismatic leader without question and take little responsibility for their actions or decisions. The dependency level of team culture is classified as dependent.

The work group, classified as the dynamic culture, is the most mature level of group development and the highest level of team culture. Open communication, creative problem solving, and synergistic learning mark this stage of group development. Members are accountable to each other, diverse views are appreciated, and team members have a resilient optimism for the future.

The Psychodynamic Perspective of Team Culture

There are numerous frameworks or lenses to view small group behavior and team dynamics. From my perspective, the psychodynamic lens is not only the most valid, it also possesses the greatest utility in creating lasting, positive change in organizations. The psychodynamic perspective focuses on the impact that the unconscious has on human behavior. In the broadest sense, the psychodynamic approach for understanding group behavior can be classified into two categories: psychoanalytic and humanistic (McLeod and Kettner-Polley, 2004). The psychoanalytic approach falls under the *medical* metaphor, with an emphasis on diagnosis and description. In this camp, the works of Sigmund Freud (1950), Wilfred Bion (1961), and Carl Jung (1912) are paramount. The humanistic approach falls under the *developmental* metaphor, with an emphasis on learning and prescription. In this camp, the works of Kurt Lewin (1945), Abraham Maslow (1954), and again Carl Jung (1912), are the most influential. The ATP represents an effort to synthesize both the psychoanalytical and humanistic approaches, taking the best from each, in order to create an engaging simulation that illustrates both diagnosis (psychoanalytic) and development (humanistic) processes in group settings.

Any discussion of psychodynamic theories must start with the founder of psychoanalysis, Sigmund Freud. Although Freud is most famous for his conception of the id, the ego, and the superego, he actually studied group behavior early in his career. Freud viewed groups as primitive collectivities grounded in extreme and irrational emotions. Unable to hold two competing ideas at the same time, or to appreciate ambiguity or the grey area that is very much a part of the human experience, especially in organizational life, groups, Freud stated, were capable of only two emotions: love (often without measure) and hate (often without reason). His distinction between the id and the ego would greatly influence Wilfred Bion's work in group behavior, discussed in more detail shortly. One of Freud's famous students and later a well-known clinician and writer in her own right, Melanie Klein (2002), expanded Freud's work in groups to help explain how the mature and conscious ego, when manifested at the group level, corresponds to reality-seeking behaviors and rational problem solving. Likewise, when the id manifests at the group level, neurotic behaviors and psychological regression, including projection and repression, emerge as protective mechanisms for the group.

Swiss psychologist Carl Jung also explored group level behavior. And like Freud, he was convinced that groups existed, psychologically at least, to avoid reality and sustain their existence on illusions. In fact, Jung famously said that when "one hundred clever heads join together in a group, one big nincompoop is the result." That's about as blunt as you can get. At a much broader level, Jung was enamored by the notion of the collective shadow, which would include not only a team and organization, but in fact entire regions, nations, and ultimately, all of humanity. Irrespective of the focus being on the individual or the group, they were united in the finding that confrontation—awareness, acknowledgment, and integration—was crucial if individuals and teams were going to realize their highest potential.

This brings us to Wilfred Bion, arguably the most influential thinker, researcher, and writer in small group behavior and the concept of team culture. Not only did Bion agree with Freud and Jung that the unconscious was a crucial part of group life, he was able to classify and categorize the collective shadow found in groups. Wilfred Bion's seminal work in group behavior is predicated on the unconscious and underlying emotionality of the groups.

According to Bion, groups simultaneously operate in two distinct states. One state is conscious, grounded in reality, and focused on the group's official task. Bion referred to this element of group behavior as the work group. The second level, which is unconscious and grounded in negative fantasy, is covert. Bion referred to this group dynamic as the basic assumption group. These two different levels always coexist together to some degree in every group. When the basic assumption group becomes dominant, the group loses touch with reality and begins to operate on tacit (as-if) assumptions grounded in emotion.

Figure H.1 illustrates the influence of Bionic terms in relation to the ATP scales and their corresponding underlying emotionality.

Basic Assumption	Underlying Group Emotion or State	ATP Scale
Fight/Flight	Apathy and Anger	Detached
Pairing	Hope and Frustration	Dramatic
Dependency	Fear and Anxiety	Dependent
Work	Passion and Authenticity	Dynamic

Figure H.1. Bionic terms in relation to ATP scales and corresponding emotionality

Using a Bionic framework for describing small group behavior and team culture has been discussed, but it may be helpful to illustrate the concept of culture. Team culture is defined as *the perceived attitude and group dynamic that results from the dynamic interplay between the overt task and the collective group shadow.* Culture emerges as the result of this dynamic tension and exists at two levels: (1) Conscious actions (visible) and (2) Shadow assumptions (invisible). Moreover, teams consider questions concerning "*What* do we need to accomplish?" and "*When* is the deliverable due?" primarily in the conscious element of group life. Questions related to "*How* are we working as a team?" and "*Why* are we working together?" occur more in the shadow or unconscious realm of group behavior. Finally, the 5 dimensions of teamwork are illustrated as they relate to this two-level distinction. The dimensions of communication, conflict management, and engagement occur primarily in the conscious or visible realm, while the dimensions of purpose and trust exist primarily below the conscious level, in the shadow or invisible realm. Figure H.2 illustrates the ATP conceptualization of team culture.

In this conceptualization, there are three unique aspects to culture: (1) Observable behaviors and artifacts above the surface of the water; (2) Dimensional norms and values that guide behavior exist both above and below the surface of the water; and (3) Collective shadow of the group that is unconscious and operates on a tacit (as-if) level.

» **Observable behaviors and artifacts**: The patterns of communication, decision-making, and conflict management

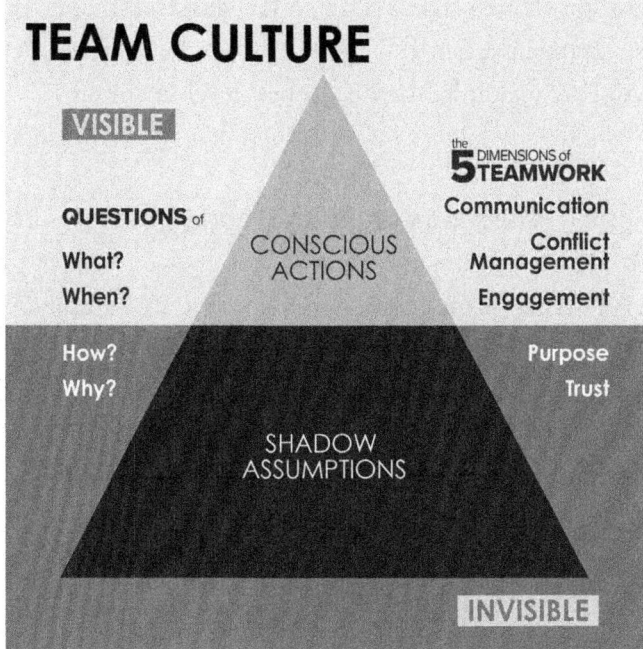

Figure H.2. ATP and team culture

processes that are unique to a team, as well as what behaviors are rewarded or reinforced, and what behaviors are punished or ignored. Artifacts include the team's logo, mission statement, dress code, and formal hierarchy that resides within the team.

» **Dimensional norms and values**: The unwritten rules of engagement that reinforce expectations, including the more deeply held convictions about what is good, bad, desirable, undesirable, and the like. The 5 dimensions of teamwork exist both above (communication, conflict management, and engagement) and below (purpose and trust) the surface. Essentially, these elements of culture are made explicit when rationales and justifications for certain acts are used and decisions are made.

» **Collective shadow**: The deepest level of culture that is unconscious and can be surfaced only through deep discovery, vulnerability, and awareness. The tacit or "as-if" assumptions about the team and its larger environment reside here, and they lead to group behavior that is often in reaction to someone or something. Primal issues such as scarcity, abundance, fear, safety, and survival are grounded in this deepest level of culture.

Validation of the ATP Long-Form

The ATP provides a measure of team culture that results from the underlying emotionality of a group based on Bion's theoretical framework. The survey contains five survey items for each of the four scales for a total of twenty items. There are five survey items that assess the 5 dimensions of teamwork, and the ATP survey concludes with an open-ended question asking for additional comments on the team's performance. The survey items by scale follow.

The Detached Scale

There is little interest in getting the job done.
Members are hostile towards each other.
Some members do not attend meetings.
We tend to drift off task.
Some members do not participate.

The Dramatic Scale

Some members want to be accepted by the group at any cost.
We are more concerned about maintaining harmony that in getting work done.
We ignore obvious problems.
We are unrealistically optimistic about our future.
We are sometimes guilty of setting unrealistic goals.

The Dependent Scale

We are unable to manage our time effectively.
We often ask for guidance.

We wait to be told what to do.
Our leader tends to know what's best for us.
We often appeal to our leader for direction.

The Dynamic Scale

Members appreciate different opinions.
We are effective listeners.
We communicate directly and honestly with each other.
We usually provide thoughtful feedback to each other.
New ideas are expressed freely.

The ATP also measures five dimensions or characteristics of high performing teams. These items are not Likert-type scale, but rather allow the participant to allocate up to ten points for each dimension based on the perceived quality of the group. In the ATP, a 10 equals exceptional or very strong on a given dimension, whereas a 1 equals poor or very low in this area. The five dimensions are

» Communication,
» Conflict management,
» Engagement,
» Purpose, and
» Trust.

The ATP has been administered to thousands of individuals in group and team settings in a variety of organizations, including business corporations, academia, non-profit and religious organizations, and governmental agencies. Appropriate sample size varies. The minimum number to meet the definition of a group is three. The most important criterion in determining the group size is whether or not the group sees itself as a group. If not, subgroups most likely exist in the larger group context and the ATP should be given separately to each subgroup within the larger department, division, or team.

The Scale Development Process

Designing and constructing an attitude assessment scale consists of three general stages: design, development, and evaluation (Schwab 1980). The theoretical framework and literature review was presented to provide the general developmental foundation of the ALP. Within the three broad stages of constructing an attitude assessment scale, Hinkin (1998) identified six steps in the scale development process. These six steps are presented in Table H.1.

Item generation is the essential first step in developing a new Likert-type scale. The primary concern during this initial stage is content validity, which should be built into the scale through the development of clear, unambiguous, and accurate items that "adequately capture the specific domain of interest" (Hinkin 1998).

It is during the initial design step that a researcher should understand the theoretical foundation that provides the basis for the scale's development. This study fell under the deductive approach to scale development because the theoretical foundation being used to define ATP provided enough information to generate an initial set of items. The major advantage of the deductive approach to scale development is that, if done properly, this approach helps to ensure content validity (Hinkin 1995).

Survey administration is the second step of the Likert-type scale development process. During this stage of scale development, the items that were retained during the content validation assessment

Table H.1. Six steps of the scale development process

Scale Development Process	
Step 1	Item Generation
Step 2	Questionnaire Administration
Step 3	Initial Item Reduction
Step 4	Confirmatory Factor Analysis
Step 5	Convergent/Discriminant Validity
Step 6	Replication

were administered to a pilot sample to confirm expectations of the psychometric properties of the new measure. Critical issues regarding scale development during this step included choosing a representative pilot sample, the sample size, and the total number of items in the new measure. These and other scaling issues are discussed in the reliability and validity sections of this paper.

Following the initial survey administration, the third step in the process of developing a Likert-type scale is the initial item reduction. Once preliminary data has been collected from the pilot sample, factor analysis was employed to further refine the scale. PCFA with orthogonal rotation is the most widely used factoring method for item reduction (Hinkin 1995). Although no absolute cutoff exists for determining which items should remain on a given scale, that is which items most clearly represent the content domain of the underlying construct, a .40 criterion level is most commonly used to judge factor loadings as meaningful (Hinkin 1998). PCFA was also used to determine the latent dimensions of the ALP framework, and a minimal eigenvalue of 1.0 was used as an appropriate criterion for retaining each dimension of the ATP assessment scale.

Once validity was established through PCFA, internal consistency should be established. Cronbach's alpha is the more widely accepted and utilized technique for establishing internal reliability and is the recommended statistic when employing PCFA (Cortina 1993).

The final two stages, assessing convergent and discriminant validity and replication, although critical to a scale's ultimate utility, are beyond the scope of this study. Convergent and discriminant validity are measures of criterion-related validity, the ability to predict a change in certain variables based on data from the predictor variable. Although this may be of eventual interest for the scale's utility, only face validity, content validity, and construct validity were ascertained for this investigation. Likewise, the final step, replication, is a time-consuming process that often takes years to establish (Hinkin, 1998). Preliminary data on replication reliability and validity will be gathered during the subsequent administrations of the

ATP, as well as efforts to predict performance, job satisfaction, and intrinsic satisfaction (e.g., the correlation of actualized leader behaviors with individual and group performance, etc.). For the current investigation, validity was assessed using PCFA to determine both the underlying structure and the number of factors explaining the observed variance (eigenvalues ≥ 1.00), and PCFA was employed to determine survey item retention ($\geq .40$) for the five items per scale with the highest R^2.

Limitations of the Research Methodology

Likert-type scales offer a range of responses with different intensities from 'strongly agree' to 'strongly disagree.' Each participant has a different interpretation of the response categories, which can lead to a degree of imprecision in the response set, data collection, and data analysis. Previous researchers have commented that Likert-type scales are akin to tape measures that stretch or contract which can, and does, impact the precision of the data collected.

The study design has limited generalizability due to homogeneous samples used for data collection. Although the sample size is beyond the recommended size of 200 (n=248), the sample was non-random and somewhat homogeneous (all members of the same organization). Additionally, the problems of social desirability and bias are limitations when using self-report measures. Social desirability, the tendency to answer questions in a manner the respondent believes that they should be answered, as opposed to the way the respondent actually believes, creates bias and error in the data analysis.

There are limitations related to validity as well. First and foremost, this research design does not afford a measure of criterion-related validity. Ultimately, one would want to be able to predict a group's performance based on the survey score. For example, are certain leadership styles, such as an actualized asserter, more effective than others with different challenges and tasks? Future research will need to establish criterion-related validity. Moreover, PCFA provides limited construct validity information due to the subjective nature of its statistical measures.

Study Sample Demographics

Before reviewing the validity and reliability analyses findings, the descriptive statistics for the current investigation are presented. First, the data was collected from a variety of organizations representing financial services, manufacturing, healthcare, and professional sports, as well as Master of Business Administration (MBA) students at an Association to Advance Collegiate Schools of Business (AACSB)-accredited comprehensive university in Charlotte, NC.

Data for the survey administration sample were captured over a six month period from June to December, 2001. During this time, 248 participants working in applied team settings completed the ATP as part of team development sessions. Table H.2 summarizes the sample's demographics.

Assessing Validity

Validity was assessed for the ATP using PFCA, a statistical technique used for exploratory data analysis. The underlying assumption of exploratory data analysis is that the more one knows about the data, the more effectively and efficiently one can develop, test, and refine a given theory, or in this case, a measurement instrument (Hartwig and Dearing 1979). Exploratory data analysis describes and summarizes data by grouping together correlated variables in factors, labeled "components," that are independent of each other (Hartwig and Dearing 1979). These components are often rotated to maximize the variance explained by each factor (Litwin 1995).

Principal Components Factor Analysis

PFCA is a statistical technique that linearly transforms an original set of variables into a substantially smaller set of uncorrelated variables. This process identifies the relevant factors under study

Table H.2. Sample demographics

Demographic Characteristics Study Sample	
Characteristic	**Percentage (%)**
Gender	
Male	31
Female	65
Missing Data	<u>4</u>
	100
Age	
20–30	44
31–40	32
41–50	10
51–60	5
61 and over	2
Missing Data	<u>7</u>
	100
Professional Experience	
1–5 Years	43
6–10 Years	24
11–15 Years	21
Over 15 Years	8
Missing Data	<u>4</u>
	100

(Dunteman 1989). PCFA is an appropriate statistical technique when the underlying factor structure is unknown. The goal of PCFA is data reduction, allowing the researcher to better understand and interpret data collected from a smaller set of uncorrelated variables (Dunteman 1989).

There are several guidelines and requirements for using PCFA. There are numerous strategies for determining how many latent factors exist in a data set and for ascertaining which survey items should be retained.

Assessing the Latent Structure of the Data Set

Determining the number of factors, or components, to retain depends on both the underlying theory and the quantitative results of the research endeavor (Hinkin 1998). Several guidelines have been established to assist researchers in making decisions about the number of latent factors to retain.

Perhaps the most well-known rule of thumb in survey development is Kaiser's Criterion. Kaiser's Criterion (also known as Kaiser's Rule) states that only components with eigenvalues that are greater than 1.0 should qualify for retention. An eigenvalue is the total amount of variance explained by a factor, and it represents the sum of the squared loadings of each variable for that factor (Hinkin 1998).

Another guide for determining the number of factors to retain in a PCFA is the scree plot test. The scree is defined as the rubble or valley where the graph plotting the factors begins to level off, and it is a graphically illustrated plot in the data set. As successive factors are extracted, and their contribution to explaining the observed variance decreases, the graph declines. The point of interest is where the curve connecting the points starts to flatten out. It is at this point where a valley or scree appears in the graph and where factor retention may stop (Kinnear and Gray 1999).

In addition to using the Kaiser Criterion and scree plot test to decide on the number of factors to retain, the underlying theory or model guiding the research should also direct factor retention decisions so long as the data set is consistent with the model in use (Hinkin 1998). That is, the research findings should fit the underlying theoretical framework in a conceptually sound way. The findings for the present study do fit the ATP framework and the conceptual models of small group behavior and team culture as defined by Wilfred Bion, and a combination of the Kaiser Criterion and the ATP theoretical framework was used to determine the number of latent factors to retain and the four-factor solution presented in Table H.3.

Latent Structure Assessment and Item Retention Analysis
PCFA of the measurement items was conducted from the data collected from the 248 surveys collected. An orthogonal (varimax) rotation was used to compute a loading matrix that represented the relationship between the observed variables and each factor. Initial

Table H.3. PCFA four-factor solution

Component 1	Detached
Component 2	Dynamic
Component 3	Dramatic
Component 4	Dependent

PCFA statistics indicated the presence of four factors (i.e., components or dimensions of motive need leadership) with eigenvalues greater than 1.0 that accounted for 42.33 percent of the total variance observed. The remaining 57.67 percent of variance from the data set was not accounted for and was assumed to lie with factors not measured by the assessment instrument. Table H.4 presents the four-component solution and resulting eigenvalues and cumulative observed variance explained by the four-factor model.

Table H.4. Cumulative variance

Component	Initial Eigenvalues			Rotation Sums of Squared Loadings		
	Total	% of Variance	Cumulative %	Total	% of Variance	Cumulative %
1	14.130	28.260	28.260	6.730	13.463	13.463
2	3.758	7.517	35.776	5.473	10.946	24.406
3	2.979	5.957	41.734	4.7549	9.507	33.913
4	1.990	3.981	45.714	4.206	8.412	42.326

Assessing Validity: Content and Construct Validity

Both content and construct validity have been established for the ATP using Pearson Correlational Coefficients (2-tailed tests) and a PCFA for construct validity. Table H.5 illustrates the range of the Pearson coefficients for the factor loadings generated using PCFA.

Table H.5. Factor loading scale component ranges

Detached	.509–.708
Dramatic	.563–.838
Dependent	.507–.674
Dynamic	.542–.720

Estimating Reliability

Coefficient alpha, commonly referred to as Cronbach's alpha and designated with "α," is a measure of internal consistency that estimates how well items hang together. Reliability is a necessary condition for validity (Hinkin 1998). In survey development, coefficient alpha measures the homogeneity of items for a given scale. Although there are other forms of reliability that can be estimated in survey research (Spector 1992), coefficient alpha is a necessary estimate for scale development and the recommended reliability statistic when computing PCFA. The overall reliability estimates for each of the five scales of group culture are presented in Table H.6, and the specific statistical output for each scale follows. Reliability estimates were calculated for each scale of the Group Culture Assessment Scale in an iterative fashion. First, coefficient alphas were calculated for all ten items of each scale. Then, internal consistency was estimated for the total number

Table H.6. Reliability assessment

Reliability Assessment Cronbach's Alpha			
Scale	Cronbach's Alpha	Cronbach's Alpha Based on Standardized Items	*N* of Items
Detached	0.8673	0.8808	5
Dramatic	0.6360	0.8235	5
Dependent	0.5146	0.7062	5
Dynamic	0.8457	0.8343	5

of items per scale to be retained in the survey's final version based on the PCFA assessment. The number of items retained for each scale in the survey's final version is five per scale, using a minimum reliability estimate threshold of .40. The total number of items retained for this section of the final version of the survey was twenty. Table H.6 summarizes this reliability assessment effort utilizing Cronbach's alpha.

Reliability Assessment for the Detached Scale

The detached scale possessed a total reliability of α = .881. Coefficient alpha was computed for the five items retained for this scale. The factor loadings ranged from .509 to .708 (exceeding the .40 recommendation). Cronbach's alpha decreased if any of the items were deleted, and the .40 minimum threshold established by Hinkin was used to make item retention decisions.

Reliability Assessment for the Dramatic Scale

The dramatic scale possessed a total reliability of α = .824. Coefficient alpha was computed for the five items retained for this scale. The factor loadings ranged from .563 to .838 (exceeding the .40 recommendation). Cronbach's alpha decreased if any of the items were deleted, and the .40 minimum threshold established by Hinkin was used to make item retention decisions.

Reliability Assessment for the Dependent Scale

The dependent scale possessed a total reliability of α = .706. Coefficient alpha was computed for the five items retained for this scale. The factor loadings ranged from .507 to .674 (exceeding the .40 recommendation). Cronbach's alpha decreased if any of the items were deleted, and the .40 minimum threshold established by Hinkin was used to make item retention decisions.

Reliability Assessment for the Dynamic Scale

The dynamic scale possessed a total reliability of α = .834. Coefficient alpha was computed for the five items retained for this scale. The factor loadings ranged from .542 to .720 (exceeding the .40 recommendation). Cronbach's alpha decreased if any of the items were deleted, and the .40 minimum threshold established by Hinkin was used to make item retention decisions.

Validation of the ATP Short-Form

The ATP short-form (free ATP) is based on the original word-pairs validated in the *Actualized Leader Profile* (ALP) (see Sparks [2019] *Technical Statement: Reliability and Validity for the ALP*). The correlation between leader style and team culture is using the ALP/ ATP short-form established in the following sections of this report.

There are twenty scale component (i.e., factor) words in ten word pairs that account for five items per scale. The ATP short-form assessment scale requires the participant to choose the word from the word-pair that is most descriptive of themselves. The ATP short-form explicitly connects leader style to team culture, and this assessment produces a graphic image that both describes leader style, and the impact of style (both good [actualized] and bad [shadow]) on team culture. See the following section of this technical statement to view the correlational coefficients between leader style and team culture. Cronbach's alphas for all five items were in the acceptable to good ranges (see Table H.7).

Table H.7. Word pairs

Word Pairs Cronbach's Alpha			
Scale	Cronbach's Alpha	Cronbach's Alpha Based on Standardized Items	*N* of Items
Achievement	.755	.753	5
Affiliation	.818	.819	5
Power	.813	.810	5
Self-Actualization	.856	.830	5

Reliability Assessment for the Word Pair Achievement Scale

The achievement scale possessed a total reliability of α = .755. Coefficient alpha was computed for the five items retained for this scale. Item analysis indicated that the retained items had moderate to strong inter-item correlations ranging from .331 to .551 (see Table H.8). Cronbach's alpha decreased if any of the items were deleted (see Table H.9).

Table H.8. Word pair achievement scale: Inter-item correlation matrix

Word Pair Achievement Scale Inter-Item Correlation Matrix					
	winning	reserved	expertise	perfection	tactical
winning	1.000	.423	.408	.331	.190
reserved	.423	1.000	.551	.471	.302
expertise	.408	.551	1.000	.428	.373
perfection	.331	.471	.428	1.000	.279
tactical	.190	.302	.373	.279	1.000

Table H.9. Word pair achievement scale: Item-total statistics

Word Pair Achievement Scale Item-Total Statistics				
	Scale Mean if Item Deleted	Scale Variance if Item Deleted	Corrected Item-Total Correlation	Squared Multiple Correlation	Cronbach's Alpha if Item Deleted
winning	13.95	195.212	.460	.234	.731
reserved	14.41	180.523	.622	.404	.671
expertise	13.32	174.542	.622	.400	.669
perfection	13.39	186.000	.520	.282	.709
tactical	15.42	217.192	.378	.163	.754

Reliability Assessment for the Word Pair Affiliation Scale

The affiliation scale possessed a total reliability of α = .818. Coefficient alpha was computed for the five items retained for this scale. Item analysis indicated that the retained items had moderate to strong inter-item correlations ranging from .411 to .609 (see Table H.10). Cronbach's alpha decreased if any of the items were deleted (see Table H.11).

Table H.10. Word pair affiliation scale: Inter-item correlation matrix

	empathy	relationships	caring	warm	mercy
empathy	1.000	.580	.542	.429	.411
relationships	.580	1.000	.609	.497	.454
caring	.542	.609	1.000	.460	.436
warm	.429	.497	.460	1.000	.324
mercy	.411	.454	.436	.324	1.000

Word Pair Affiliation Scale Inter-Item Correlation Matrix

Table H.11. Word pair affiliation scale: Item-total statistics

	Scale Mean if Item Deleted	Scale Variance if Item Deleted	Corrected Item-Total Correlation	Squared Multiple Correlation	Cronbach's Alpha if Item Deleted
empathy	24.26	223.474	.634	.416	.775
relationships	24.57	212.902	.705	.507	.753
caring	24.34	218.896	.668	.459	.764
warm	24.39	234.067	.538	.303	.802
mercy	26.08	232.754	.508	.266	.812

Word Pair Affiliation Scale Item-Total Statistics

Reliability Assessment for the Word-Pair Power Scale

The power scale possessed a total reliability of $\alpha = .813$. Coefficient alpha was computed for the five items retained for this scale. Item analysis indicated that the retained items had moderate to strong inter-item correlations ranging from .172 to .771 (see Table H.12). Cronbach's alpha decreased if any of the items were deleted (see Table H.13).

Table H.12. Word pair power scale: Inter-item correlation matrix

Word Pair Power Scale Inter-Item Correlation Matrix					
	justice	strategic	power	control	results
justice	1.000	.370	.388	.588	.771
strategic	.370	1.000	.172	.229	.464
power	.388	.172	1.000	.248	.362
control	.588	.229	.248	1.000	.647
results	.771	.464	.362	.647	1.000

Table H.13. Word pair power scale: Item-total statistics

Word Pair Power Scale Item-Total Statistics					
	Scale Mean if Item Deleted	Scale Variance if Item Deleted	Corrected Item-Total Correlation	Squared Multiple Correlation	Cronbach's Alpha if Item Deleted
justice	18.40	183.938	.743	.621	.694
strategic	16.97	230.472	.395	.226	.809
power	21.64	248.358	.369	.160	.810
control	18.28	202.505	.579	.445	.753
results	18.99	177.882	.805	.690	.671

Reliability Assessment for the Word-Pair Self-Actualization Scale

The self-actualization scale possessed a total reliability of $\alpha = .856$. Coefficient alpha was computed for the five items retained for this scale. Item analysis indicated that the retained items had moderate to strong inter-item correlations ranging from .123 to .828 (see Table H.14). Cronbach's alpha decreased if any of the items were deleted (see Table H.15).

Validation of the Actualized Performance Cube: Leader Style and Team Culture

The actualized performance cube is presented as an evidence-based model that connects leader style (as measured by the ALP) to team culture (as measured by the ATP). The findings indicate statistically significant correlational relationships between all four hypothesized relationships, which follow in Figure H.3.

Researchers in applied and organizational settings have long examined the impact of leader and managerial style on team culture (Lewin 1945; Quinn 1988; Sparks 2002). Recent efforts in both research (Pieri 2022) and more popular press such as *Stanford Business* (Kim 2023) have examined the impact of leader style and

Table H.14. Word pair self-actualization scale: Inter-item correlation matrix

Word Pair Self-Actualization Scale Inter-Item Correlation Matrix					
	risk	spontaneous	candor	trust	creativity
risk	1.000	.828	.378	.254	.746
spontaneous	.828	1.000	.425	.266	.780
candor	.378	.425	1.000	.123	.342
trust	.254	.266	.123	1.000	.114
creativity	.746	.780	.342	.114	1.000

Table H.15. Word pair self-actualization scale: Item-total statistics

Word Pair Self-Actualization Scale Item-Total Statistics					
	Scale Mean if Item Deleted	Scale Variance if Item Deleted	Corrected Item-Total Correlation	Squared Multiple Correlation	Cronbach's Alpha if Item Deleted
risk	22.10	166.280	.812	.717	.673
spontaneous	21.92	161.801	.856	.767	.655
candor	23.26	222.064	.359	.246	.825
trust	17.80	270.319	.157	.173	.851
creativity	21.86	174.476	.728	.653	.704

Achiever Leader Style	>	Detached Team Culture
Affirmer Leader Style	>	Dramatic Team Culture
Asserter Leader Style	>	Dependent Team Culture
Actualized Leader Style	>	Dynamic Team Culture

Figure H.3. Statistically significant correlational relationships personality on team and company culture. The current section of this technical report is focused on providing the research methodology and findings that establish the correlations between leader style and team culture as reported by Pieri (2022).

The four leader styles that emerge in the ALP Framework can be plotted on two dimensions: orientation and problem-solving. Orientation refers to mindset and focus of the leader. The ALP Framework illustrates task orientation based on the underlying motive need driving the leader's style. There are two distinct approaches that emerge: tactical and strategic. A more tactical orientation is a short-term, execution-focused approach that may be best described as rational, pragmatic, tangible, planned, practical, and cautious. The achiever and affirmer styles are more tactical. A more strategic orientation is a long-term, results-focused approach that may be best described as big-picture, holistic, imaginative, spontaneous, objective, and risky. The asserter and actualized styles are more strategic.

The second dimension is based on problem-solving and decision-making. There are two basic approaches that emerge: logical and intuitive. A more logical approach to problem-solving favors rationality, data, predictability, sensibility, process, and procedure. The achiever and asserter styles are more logical. A more intuitive approach to problem-solving favors inference, novelty, gut-feel, sixth sense, imagination, and play. The affirmer and actualized styles are more intuitive. Figure 2.2 provides a summary overview of the four approaches to leadership plotted on the two dimensions of orientation and problem-solving, yielding a 2×2 matrix.

Team culture is created and sustained from three primary forces: the leader's style and shadow, the styles of the individual members, and the broader context in which the team is operating. Of these three, research suggests that the leader has the greatest impact—for good or for ill—on their team's culture and performance.

Similar to the leadership styles, another 2×2 matrix for team culture can be created (see Figure 2.3). But, more importantly, it can also be mapped onto Figure 2.4 as an extension of leader style. As such, in Figure 2.4 you can visually see what I refer to as the actualized performance cube, which illustrates the connection between leader style and culture.

The team culture matrix is based on two dimensions: performance and results, and people and relationships. Performance and results refers to the overall effectiveness of the team in accomplishing goals and productivity, classified as either low or high. The detached and dramatic cultures tend to perform at lower levels, while the dependent and dynamic cultures tend to perform at higher levels.

The second dimension is people and relationships and this refers to the overall engagement and connection that team members experience intrinsically, also classified as either low or high. The detached and dependent cultures are cooler and tend to have members that are less engaged and satisfied. The dramatic and dynamic cultures are warmer and tend to have members that are more engaged and satisfied.

Pieri (2022) established the statistically significant correlations between the ALP leader styles and ATP team cultures. This model, the actualized performance cube, links the two previously illustrated 2×2 matrices of leader style and team culture into one comprehensive framework. This section provides an overview of the research methodology and findings related to these hypothesized relationship. Figure 2.4 illustrates the actualized performance cube.

This research study was conducted in 2021–2022 and assessed 15 intact teams with a sample size of 113 participants. The data were collected from a population of team leaders and individual members from the leaders' teams. Team leaders and team members came from several workplace organizations that featured intact teams with a team's designated leader. The organizations represented different for-profit and non-profit sectors of the workplace, including a law firm, a healthcare institution, financial institutions (both a large national bank and a small local bank), a national retail chain, a pharmaceutical company, a professional sports team, and a global marketing firm. Sampling for the study was convenience sampling. Although the subjects came from convenience sampling, the sample provides relevant information for addressing the study's research questions. The following teams participated in the study, including their industry and the total number of participants from the team, including the leader:

1. Global manufacturing firm (six participants).
2. National retail chain (eight participants).
3. Health care (eight participants).
4. Law (six participants).
5. Healthcare (six participants).
6. National bank (twenty participants).
7. Professional sports (six participants).
8. National bank (eight participants).
9. Healthcare (twelve participants).
10. National bank (six participants).
11. Local bank (four participants).
12. National bank (six participants).
13. National bank (six participants).
14. National bank (four participants).
15. National retail pharmacy chain (six participants).

The research question driving this examination follows: *To what extent, if any, does leader style and team culture correlate?* Table H.16 shows the number of team members and leaders who participated in the study along with the ALP and ATP scores for the study participants. Higher ALP scores ranging from 0 to 100 indicate a greater self-assessment of self-actualization, being less reactive under stress and possessing a greater sense of self-awareness. Team size ranged from a low of four to a high of twenty, both within the three to twenty-four membership size defined as the acceptable parameters for the current study. Over half the teams (eight) contained six members. The ALP had a wider range of scores than the ATP (82 versus 69).

Table H.16. Team sizes and profile scores

Team Sizes and Profile Scores			
Group	Size of team	ALP score	ATP score
1	6	92	77
2	8	66	83
3	8	64	86
4	6	17	27
5	6	96	52
6	20	99	96
7	6	81	70
8	8	30	76
9	12	81	84
10	6	56	80
11	4	32	83
12	6	98	82
13	6	46	90
14	4	86	75
15	6	41	71

Note. ALP = Actualized Leader Profile. ATP = Actualized Team Profile.

Table H.17 shows the range, minimum, maximum, means, and standard deviations of the ALP and ATP scores for the 113 participants of this study. The data show the ATP scores had a higher average than the ALP scores (75.04 versus 68.36). However, the

Table H.17. Descriptive statistics for response data

Descriptive Statistics for Response Data						
Item	No.*	Range	Min.	Max.	Mean	SD
ALP	113	82	17	99	68.36	24.88
ATP	113	69	27	96	75.04	15.70

*Valid N = 113. ALP = Actualized Leader Profile. ATP = Actualized Team Profile.

ALP had a wider range of scores than the ATP (82 versus 69) and a greater standard deviation (24.88 versus 15.70). Overall, the ALP scores contained more variance than the ATP scores.

Detached Culture and the Achiever Style

Table H.18 shows the achiever scores and the detached culture scores for the fifteen groups that participated in the current study. Team size ranged from a low of four to a high of twenty, both within the three to twenty-four membership size that Bion defined as the acceptable parameters from his research. Over half the teams (eight) contained six members. The achiever scores contained greater variance, as shown by the broader range of scores (88 to 31).

Table H.18. Team sizes with achiever style and detached culture scores

Team Sizes With Achiever Style and Detached Culture Scores			
Group	Size of team	Achiever	Detached
1	6	8	14
2	8	50	2
3	8	68	2
4	6	91	25
5	6	8	2
6	20	38	2
7	6	3	7
8	8	91	33
9	12	50	2
10	6	14	5
11	4	50	3
12	6	18	7
13	6	27	2
14	4	14	17
15	6	38	38

Table H.19 shows the range, minimum, maximum, means, and standard deviations for the achiever and detached culture scores.

The data show the achiever and detached culture means had a large difference, with the achiever mean being higher than the detached culture mean (37.49 versus 8.83). The achiever scores contained greater variance, as shown by the broader range of scores (88 to 31) and higher standard deviation (26.75 versus 11.03).

Table H.19. Descriptive statistics for achiever scores and detached culture scores

Descriptive Statistics for Achiever Scores and Detached Culture Scores						
Item	No.*	Range	Min.	Max.	Mean	SD
Achiever	113	88	3	91	37.49	26.75
Detached	113	31	2	93	8.83	11.03

*Valid $N = 113$.

Table H.20 shows the Pearson correlation between achiever scores and detached culture scores. There was a statistically significant correlation between the achiever scores and the detached culture scores, $r(113) = .347$, $p < .01$. Overall, the leaders' need for achievement is positively related to teams' detached scores.

Table H.20. Pearson's correlation between achiever scores and the detached culture scores

Pearson's Correlation Between Achiever Scores and the Detached Culture Scores		
Item	Achiever	Detached
Pearson correlation	1	.347*
Sig. (2-tailed)		< .001
No.	113	113

*$p < .01$.

Dramatic Culture and the Affirmer Style

Table H.21 shows the affirmer scores and the dramatic culture scores for the fifteen groups that participated in the current study. Team size ranged from a low of four to a high of twenty, both within the three to twenty-four membership size parameters that are defined as the acceptable for the current study. Over half the teams (eight) contained six members. The affirmer scores had a greater amount of variance as shown by a wider range of scores (83 to 60).

Table H.21. Team sizes with affirmer and dramatic culture scores

Team Sizes with Affirmer and Dramatic Culture Scores			
Group	Size of team	Affirmer	Dramatic
1	6	71	41
2	8	8	22
3	8	2	11
4	6	23	66
5	6	11	58
6	20	78	15
7	6	85	26
8	8	2	35
9	12	2	28
10	6	67	28
11	4	78	23
12	6	19	14
13	6	75	6
14	4	19	43
15	6	19	62

Table H.22 shows the descriptive statistics for leader affirmer scores and dramatic culture scores. The data show the affirmer and dramatic culture means had a very small difference, with the affirmer mean being slightly higher than the dramatic culture scores mean (30.53 versus 29.58). The affirmer scores had a greater amount of variance as shown by a wider range of scores (83 to 60) and a higher standard deviation (32.53 versus 15.91).

Table H.22. Descriptive statistics for affirmer scores and dramatic culture scores

Descriptive Statistics for Affirmer Scores and Dramatic Culture Scores						
Item	No.*	Range	Min.	Max.	Mean	SD
Affirmer	113	83	2	85	30.53	32.53
Dramatic	113	60	6	66	29.58	15.91

*Valid $N = 113$.

Table H.23 shows the Pearson correlation between affirmer scores and dramatic culture scores. There was a statistically significant correlation between the affirmer scores and the dramatic culture scores, $r(113) = 186$, $p < .05$. The affirmer and dramatic scores were correlated.

Table H.23. Pearson's correlation between affirmer scores and the dramatic culture scores

Pearson's Correlation Between Affirmer Scores and the Dramatic Culture Scores		
Item	Affirmer	Dramatic
Pearson correlation	1	.186*
Sig. (2-tailed)		.0049
No.	113	113

*$p < .05$.

Dependent Culture and the Asserter Style
Table H.24 provides the asserter scores and the dependent culture scores for the fifteen groups that participated in the study. Team size ranged from a low of four to a high of twenty, both within the three to twenty-four membership size that Bion defined as the acceptable parameters from his research. Over half the teams (eight) contained six members.

Table H.25 shows the descriptive statistics for asserter scores and dependent culture scores. The data show that asserter scores had a greater variance, as shown by a broader range of scores (95 to 72) than the dependent culture scores. The data show asserter and dependent culture means had a moderate difference, with the asserter mean being higher than the dependent culture scores mean (66.11 versus 52.56). The asserter scores had a greater variance, as shown by a broader range of scores (95 to 72) and a higher standard deviation (31.17 versus 14.24).

Table H.26 indicates there was a statistically significant correlation between the asserter style and the dependent culture scores, $r(113) = .489$, $p < .01$. The asserter and dependent scores were

Table H.24. Team sizes with asserter and dependent culture scores

Team Sizes With Asserter and Dependent Culture Scores			
Group	Size of team	Asserter	Dependent
1	6	18	13
2	8	96	48
3	8	99	55
4	6	82	43
5	6	74	47
6	20	4	65
7	6	11	37
8	8	91	82
9	12	94	57
10	6	22	44
11	4	59	66
12	6	59	52
13	6	59	57
14	4	59	65
15	6	88	68

Table H.25. Descriptive statistics for asserter scores and dependent culture scores

Descriptive Statistics for Asserter Scores and Dependent Culture Scores						
Item	No.*	Range	Min.	Max.	Mean	SD
Asserter	113	95	4	99	66.11	31.17
Dependent	113	72	13	85	52.56	14.24

*Valid N = 113.

Table H.26. Pearson's correlation between asserter scores and the dependent culture scores

Pearson's Correlation Between Asserter Scores and the Dependent Culture Scores		
Item	Asserter	Dependent
Pearson correlation	1	.489*
Sig. (2-tailed)		< .001
No.	113	113

*$p < .01$.

positively correlated. Overall, higher asserter scores among the leaders correlated with higher dependent culture scores.

Dynamic Culture and the Actualized Style

Table H.27 shows the actualized scores and the dynamic culture scores for the fifteen groups that participated in the current study. Team size ranged from a low of four to a high of twenty, both within the three to twenty-four membership size parameters that are defined as the acceptable for the current study.

Table H.28 shows the range, minimum, maximum, means, and standard deviations of the ALP and Actualized Team Profile (ATP) scores for the 113 participants of this study. The data show the ATP scores had a higher average than the ALP scores (75.04 versus 68.36). However, the ALP had a wider range of scores than the ATP (82 versus 69) and a greater standard deviation (24.88 versus

Table H.27. Team sizes and profile scores

Team Sizes and Profile Scores			
Group	Size of team	ALP score	ATP score
1	6	92	77
2	8	66	83
3	8	64	86
4	6	17	27
5	6	96	52
6	20	99	96
7	6	81	70
8	8	30	76
9	12	81	84
10	6	56	80
11	4	32	83
12	6	98	82
13	6	46	90
14	4	86	75
15	6	41	71

Note. ALP = Actualized Leader Profile. ATP = Actualized Team Profile.

Table H.28. Descriptive statistics for response data

Descriptive Statistics for Response Data						
Item	No.*	Range	Min.	Max.	Mean	SD
ALP	113	82	17	99	68.36	24.88
ATP	113	69	27	96	75.04	15.70

Note. ALP = Actualized Leader Profile. ATP = Actualized Team Profile.
*Valid N = 113

15.70). Overall, the ALP scores contained more variance than the ATP scores.

Table H.29 shows the Pearson correlation between the ALP and ATP scores. The data show there was a statistically significant correlation between the ALP and ATP scores, $r(113)$ = .202, $p < .05$. In addition, the ALP and ATP scores were positively correlated. Overall, higher self-actualization scores among the leaders related to higher dynamic group culture scores for the teams the leaders managed.

Table H.29. Pearson's correlation between actualized leaders and the dynamic team culture

Pearson's Correlation Between Actualized Leaders and the Dynamic Team Culture		
Item	ALP	ATP
Pearson correlation	1	.202*
Sig. (2-tailed)		.032
No.	113	113

Note. ALP = Actualized Leader Profile. ATP = Actualized Team Profile.
*$p < .05$.

Summary

The ATP is a valid and reliable self-reporting team-based assessment for measuring small group behavior and team culture based on the framework of Wilfred Bion. The steps outlined in this effort follow well-accepted guidelines for the scale development process (Hinkin 1995) and yield a four-factor model of leader style and team culture, with impressive factor loading well above the suggested .40 cutoff, which indicates that the retained survey items have a high degree of construct validity. Moreover, the scales are estimated to have a high degree of reliability. The scales' average Cronbach's alpha is .811, meaning that the consistency of the items by scale is very good. As such, it can be affirmed that the ATP is both a precise (valid) and consistent (reliable) assessment for measuring team culture based on the underlying emotionality of the group.

The ATP short-form (http://www.atpfree.com) also demonstrates well-above recommended reliability and construct validity estimates. The short-form assessment links individual style to team culture and provides a graphic measure of the impact of both optimal (actualized) and suboptimal (shadow) behaviors on creating and sustaining team culture.

Finally, the actualized performance cube findings yield statistically significant results confirming the significant correlations between leader style and team culture. These correlational coefficients occur at both the $p < .05$ level (dramatic and dynamic) and at the $p < .01$ level (detached and dependent.) As such, the actualized performance cube has been validated as a framework for understanding the inherent connection and correlation between leader style and team culture, and the resulting group dynamics and decision-making processes the occur. The implications for future research include establishing predictive validity between leader style and group culture and estimating levels of team member engagement by specific culture.

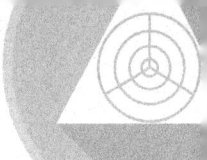

References

Badaracco, Joseph L., Jr. 2003. "Right versus Right: Dealing with Ethical Dilemmas in Business." In *How to Run a Company*, edited by Dennis C. Carey and Marie-Caroline von Weichs, 271–280. New York: Crown Business.

Bernstein, W. J. 2021. *The Delusions of Crowds: Why People Go Mad in Groups*. Grove Press.

Bion, Wilfred R. 1961. *Experiences in Groups*. New York: Basic Books.

Campbell, Joseph. 2008. *The Hero with a Thousand Faces*. 3rd ed. Novato, CA: New World Library.

Cattell, Raymond B. 1966. "The Scree Test for the Number of Factors." *Multivariate Behavioral Research* 1, no. 2: 245–276.

Collins, James. 2001. *Good to Great: Why Some Companies Make the Leap. . . and Others Don't*. New York: HarperBusiness.

Cortina, Jose M. 1993. "What is Coefficient Alpha?: An Examination of Theory and Applications." *Journal of Applied Psychology* 78: 98–104.

Dunteman, George H. 1989. *Principal Components Analysis*. Newbury Park, CA: Sage Publications, Inc.

Eisenhardt, Kathleen A., Jean L. Kahwajy, and L.J. Bourgeois III. 1997. "How Management Teams Can Have a Good Fight." *Harvard Business Review*.

Emerson, Ralph Waldo. 2020. *Emerson's Essay: The Complete First & Second Series*. New York: Skyhorse Publishing.

Freud, Sigmund. 1950). *Group Psychology and the Analysis of the Ego*. New York: Hogarth Press.

Goldsmith, Marshall. 2007. *What Got You Here Won't Get You There*. Hyperion Books.

Hartwig, Frederick, and Brian E. Dearing. 1979. *Exploratory Data Analysis.* Newbury Park, CA: Sage Publications, Inc.

Harvey, Jerry B. 1988. *The Abilene Paradox: And Other Meditations on Management.* San Franciso: Jossey-Bass Publishers.

Hayashi, Alden M. 2001. "When to Trust your Gut." *Harvard Business Review.*

Herminia, Ibarra, Claudius A. Hildebrand, and Sabine Vinck. 2023. "The Leadership Odyssey." *Harvard Business Review.*

Herzberg, Frederick. 2003. "One More Time: How Do You Motivate Employees?" *Harvard Business Review.*

Hinkin, Timothy R. 1995. "A Review of Scale Development Practices in the Study of Organizations." *Journal of Management* 21, no. 5: 967–986.

Hinkin, Timothy R. 1998. "A Brief Tutorial on the Development of Measures for Use in Survey Questionnaires." *Organizational Research Methods* 1, no. 1: 104–121.

Hoffer, Eric. 2006. *The Ordeal of Change.* Titusville, NJ: Hopewell Publications.

Janis, Irving. 1972. *Victims of Groupthink.* Boston: Houghton Mifflin Company.

Jaques, Elliott. 1965. "Death and the Mid-Life Crisis." *The International Journal of Psycho-Analysis* 46: 502–514.

Jaques, Elliott. 2006. *Requisite Organization.* 2nd ed. Falls Church, VA: Cason Hall & Co. Publishers.

Jenkins, Sally. 2023. *The Right Call: What Sports Teach Us About Work and Life.* Gallery Books.

Jung, Carl. 1912. *The Psychology of the Unconscious.* New York: Dover Publications.

Jung, Carl. 1963. *Memories, Dreams, Reflections.* New York: Pantheon Books.

Jung, Carl. 1969. *The Structure and Dynamics of the Psyche.* 2nd ed. Princeton, NJ: Princeton University Press.

Katzenbach, Jon R., and Douglas K. Smith. 2015. *The Wisdom of Teams*. Harvard Business Review Press.

Kets de Vries, Manfred, and Danny Miller. 1984. *The Neurotic Organization*. San Francisco: Jossey-Bass Publishers.

Kim, Audrey. 2023. "Follow the Leader: How CEO's Personality is Reflected in Their Company's Culture." *Stanford Business* (blog), August 1, 2023. https://www.gsb.stanford.edu/insights/follow-leader-how-ceos-personality-reflected-their-companys-culture.

Kinnear, Paul R., and Collin D. Gray. 1999. *SPSS for Windows Made Simple* (3rd ed.). East Sussex, UK: Psychology Press Ltd., Publishers.

Klein, Melanie. 2017. *Lectures on Technique*. London: Routledge.

Knowles, Jonathan, B., Tom Hunsaker, Hannah Grove, and Alison James. 2022. "What is the Purpose of your Purpose?" *Harvard Business Review*.

Lewin, Kurt. 1945. *Resolving Social Conflicts*. New York: Harper & Brothers Publishers.

Litwin, Mark S. 1995. *How to Measure Survey Reliability and Validity. The Survey Kit*. vol. 7. Thousand Oaks, CA: Sage Publications.

Maslow, Abraham. 1954. *Motivation and Personality* (3rd ed.). New York, NY: Harper & Brothers Publishers.

McCleod, Poppy L., and Richard Kettner-Polley. 2004. "Contributions of Psychodynamic Theories to Understanding Small Groups," *Small Group Research* 35, no. 3: 333–360.

Minson, Julia A., and Julia Francesca. 2022. "Managing a Polarized Workforce." *Harvard Business Review*.

Nunnally, Jum C. 1967. *Psychometric Theory*. New York, NY: McGraw-Hill.

O'Toole, James, and Warren Bennis. 2009. "A Culture of Candor." *Harvard Business Review*.

Page, Scott. 2017. *The Diversity Bonus*. Princeton University Press.

Perlow, Leslie A. 2014. "Manage Your Team's Collective Time." *Harvard Business Review.*

Pieri, Joseph. 2022. "Self-Actualized Leaders' Relationships with Dynamic Teams." Florida: Unpublished Doctoral Dissertation, Nova Southeastern University.

Quinn, Robert E. 1996. *Deep Change.* San Franciso: Jossey-Bass Publishers.

Quinn, Robert E., and Anjan V. Thakor. 2018. "Creating a Purpose-Driven Organization." *Harvard Business Review.*

Schein, Edgar. 2016. *Organizational Culture and Leadership.* 5th ed. Hoboken, NJ: John Wiley & Sons, Inc.

Schwab, Donald P. 1980. "Construct Validity in Organization Behavior." In *Research in Organizational Behavior*, edited by L. L. Cummings and Barry M. Straw. Greenwich, CT: JAI.

Schwarz, Robert M. 2013. *Smart Leaders. Smarter Teams.* Jossey-Bass.

Sparks, William L. 2002. "Measuring the Impact of Basic Assumption Mental States on Group Culture: The Design, Development and Evaluation of a Group Culture Assessment Scale." Washington, DC: Unpublished Doctoral Dissertation, The George Washington University.

Sparks, William L. 2019. *Actualized Leadership: Meeting Your Shadow & Maximizing Your Potential.* Alexandria, VA: Society for Human Resource Management Publishing.

Spector, Paul E. 1992. *Summated Rating Scale Construction: An Introduction.* Newbury Park, CA: Sage Publications, Inc.

Stein, Daniel, Nick Hobson, Jon M. Jachimowicz, and Ashley Whillans. 2021. "How Companies Can Improve Employee Engagement Right Now." *Harvard Business Review.*

Stobierski, Tim. 2020. "What Are Strategic Thinking Skills?" *Harvard Business Review.*

Stock, Dorothy, and Herbert A. Thelen. 1958. *Emotional Dynamics and Group Culture.* Washington, DC: National Training Laboratories.

Thelen, Herbert A. 1954. *Dynamics of Groups at Work.* Chicago: University of Chicago Press.

Velasquez, Luis, and Kristin Gleitsman. 2023. "How to Equip Your Team to Problem Solve Without You." *Harvard Business Review.*

Zak, Paul. 2017. "The Neuroscience of Trust." *Harvard Business Review.*

Index

organizational psychologists xiv
orientation 26, 144, 200
O'Toole, James 116, 170
output 4
over-confidence effect 63–64

P
pairing 23
paradoxical intent 38, 49, 61
patterns
    communication 18, 19
    conflict management process 18
    decision-making 18
    group behavior 11, 18
Patterson, Jerry 170
Patterson, Kathie xvi
    conflict management 123
peak performance xviii
Pearl Harbor 73
peer pressure 86, 142
performance 136
    goals 4
    group xvii
Perlow, Leslie 127
Pope John Paul II 50
pornography 3
potential xvii
    confrontation and 23
    group 16
    individual 16, 23
    team 23
"The Power of Self Awareness" 21,
    46, 143
"The Power of Vulnerability" 105
prescription 13
primal issues 18
problem-solving 4, 19, 144, 200
    Actualized Leadership Profile (ALP)
        Framework and 26
    ego and 23
pro-dependent 21
projects 5
psychoanalyst 11
psychoanalytical approach xvii, 13

psychodynamic approach xvii, 161,
    199–201
    culture 20
    definition of 16
    humanistic category 13, 22, 199
    psychoanalytic category 22, 199
psychodynamics xvi
    Actualized Teamwork Framework
        and 12
    theory of group behavior 11
psychological safety 153, 161
psychological vs. physical
    disengement 39
psychologist 11
psychopathology 9
purpose 18
    mutual 6
    personal 134
purpose (dimension 4) 130–135
    definition of 131
    individual vs. organizational 131,
        134
    statement of 131
    Team Purpose Worksheet 131, 133
    three senses of purpose 133

Q
Quinn, Robert E. 19, 130, 170

R
remote work 126
resiliency 134
responsibility 158
restraining forces 185
return 146
Rheem, Don 170
The Right Call 104

S
Salyer, Jamaree 105
San Francisco 49ers 105, 106
satisfaction 20
Savoy, Brian xvi, 134
Schein, Edgar 19

About the Author

William L. Sparks, PhD, serves as the Dennis Thompson Distinguished Chair and Professor of Leadership at the McColl School of Business at Queens University of Charlotte. Concurrently, he serves as the CEO of Actualized Performance Solutions and as the Executive Director of the Center for Human and Organizational Potential. His applied research and consulting activities focus on leader, team and board development, organizational change, and executive coaching. He created and validated the Actualized Leader Profile©, the ALP360©, and the Actualized Team Profile©, which have been translated into nine languages. He is the author of the Amazon #1 best seller *Actualized Leadership: Meeting Your Shadow & Maximizing Your Potential* (SHRM, 2019) and the coauthor (with Peter Browning) of *The Director's Manual: A Framework for Board Governance* (Wiley, 2016). His TED Talk "The Power of Self-Awareness" explores the importance of personal responsibility in the process of realizing one's full potential. He completed his PhD in Organizational Behavior and Development from the School of Business and Public Management at the George Washington University and resides in Charlotte, NC, with his wife Erin and son Bennett.